WE JEWS and YOU CHRISTIANS

Also by Samuel Sandmel

Herod: Profile of a Tyrant
The Hebrew Scriptures
We Jews and Jesus
The Genius of Paul
Philo's Place in Judaism
A Jewish Understanding of the New Testament

We Jews and You Christians:

J. B. LIPPINCOTT COMPANY

AN INQUIRY INTO ATTITUDES

---

by SAMUEL SANDMEL

PHILADELPHIA & NEW YORK

First Edition
Printed in the United States of America
Library of Congress Catalog Card No.: 67-28282

To the Reverend Sidney Lovett
Chaplain of Yale University, 1932-1958
My cherished friend for all time

TABLE OF CONTENTS

WE JEWS and YOU CHRISTIANS

1

PRELIMINARIES

This little book seeks to give an answer to a question very often put to me by Christians: What is the attitude of you Jews to us? This question frequently comes to me, openly or by suggestion, in the discussion periods following lectures I have given. The lectures ordinarily deal with some aspect of the field in which I have specialized, earliest Christianity and its relationship to the Judaism of that time, and treat matters of today only indirectly or passingly. My problem in answering the question at the moment of its asking is the lack of sufficient time to treat the matter with the respect that it deserves, and the consequent need to try to answer in generalized terms, even though manifestly there are all kinds of Christians and all kinds of Jews, and the historical, sociological, and theological factors are somewhat complicated. This book is a means whereby without haste or oversimplification I can address myself to assembling a reliable answer to an important question.

This question about attitude has seemed to me to arise more from concrete situations than from abstract ones. That is to say, there are situations such as Jewish families living in amiability to next-door Christians, and Jewish business or professional men in affirmative contact with Christians, and Jewish students with Christian roommates. In many such situations the respective human qualities emerge, so that individual Jews and individual Christians can become aware of discovering nobility or baseness, affability or irritability, social responsibility or its lack, in each other. The factor of religion, though, can either becloud these recognitions or else, through incomprehensions, or suspicions, or sensitivities, stand in the way of a fullness of mutual regard. The terms "Jew" and "Christian" in themselves imply collective entities that in some ways shape the individual. I have learned that the question, What do you Jews think of us Christians? often means most specifically, What attitude does my Jewish neighbor or associate, or roommate, have to me, not as person to person, but as Jew to Christian? To a person of good will, this consideration is a matter of real concern; to a person of ill will the question seldom if ever arises.

By now the question is not a new one, at least in the United States, and there is a large quantity of literature which sets forth to explain the religious traditions of Jews and Christians to each other. Almost invariably these explanations deal with religious holy days—what does Yom Kippur mean, or Easter—but abstain, so it seems to me, from a more profound inquiry into the habits of thought, habits of response, and the manner of the approaches, respectively, of Jews and Christians to religion. Especially noticeable is the way in which the basic theological stances of the Jew or the Christian are omitted. Indeed, one might say that such books supply data, but not the meaning of the data. It is this latter which I here attempt to supply and I try to answer the question as best I can of attitude, both in the collective sense, we Jews and you Christians, and thereby in the individual sense, the Jewish family next door, and your family.

In the very make-up of the Jewish community, neither I nor any other Jew can consider himself the official spokesman for all Jews. That being so, the personal element in the answers as I formulate them to the question, What do you Jews think of us Christians? must be noted. Another Jew might conceivably give the same answer, or he might couch a similar answer in different terms, or give a significantly different answer.

I shall do the best that I can to reflect us Jews, all of us, and also to abstain from too great an intrusion of my own dispositions and biases. I shall try to report on what Jewish attitudes are, and not just what I would personally want them to be. I will try to do justice to Jewish views which I know are different from my own.

I have thought that a short statement might well be drawn up to embody what I take to be a responsible reflection of the Jewish attitude toward Christians and Christianity. That brief statement is to be found at the close of this book. Indeed, what comes before is in a way both the prologue to that statement and, I trust, an adequate explanation of it.

Statements in this vein on Jews have come from assembled bodies of Christians. The statement of this book on a Jewish attitude toward Christians is in a sense only mine, for it comes from my pen and not from an assembled body of Jews. It comes, however, out of an inquiry into Jewish literature and a lifetime context of Jewish thought. Thus, in its essence it is a responsible Jewish statement, even though the language and the wording are the voice of one man. Only if and when the wording appeals to other Jews as a reliable and felicitous formulation, and they therefore accept it and quote it, can it become more than simply mine. Better still, other Jews may be moved to propose more appropriate formulations of this same substance.

2

HISTORICAL BACKGROUNDS

Changes in Jewish Life

When we enter, as now, the last third of the 20th century, we stand at a moment in history when much of the past—some would say all of it—is undergoing tremendous revision. I need here only to list these facets of the enormous pattern of change: the scientific developments (atomic power, space exploration, laser beams, medical innovations), the political upheavals (the birth and rise of communist states, the termination of colonialism), the deep-seated religious questioning and the cultural upheavals (such as the new sexual frankness, including the rise to the surface of homosexuality, the prevalence of divorce, new genres of art and literature). This, then, is in a large sense a time of reappraisals.

What rises to deter a person from writing a book such as this one is not alone these great changes, unsettling to premises which only recently were firm, but even more to the point, the relative recency of many drastic changes in the life of us Jews ourselves. "Recency" might to some be a misleading word, and since I prefer to continue to use it, I must clarify the meaning I here attach to it.

In the 19th century, within an abundance of human migrations, Jews were also among those who migrated. Ordinarily a migrating Jew was departing from life in a closed ghetto that had progressed but little since medieval times, and coming into a relatively open Western civilization. Thus, though there has been Jewish settlement in the United States and England for many generations, it represents only a small though significant minority of us; the bulk of us Jews in Western countries are of origin so recent that the present adult Jewish community, people in the 50's, represents largely the first Western-born generation. In this sense I personally belong to a transitional generation; my parents were born in ghettos, and I in free America, but my children are only dimly aware of these factors of difference. My experience is totally American; my language is English, not Yiddish;[1] I went to public schools (the American law compelled me to; my father, where he lived, was forbidden by law); I served for almost four years in the United States Navy in World War II. Culturally I am both in and of the United States, and this in a

[1] This language is a German dialect, with admixtures of Hebrew, and also other regional languages. Jews carried it from Germany throughout northern and eastern Europe. It uses the Hebrew alphabet.

manner far beyond the great adjustments that were incumbent on my parents on their arrival here. By recency, then, I have in mind not just my own family's situation, but also that of most of us Jews. I must emphasize too that this migration was not only from one place to another, but, as it were, from one age to another. That is to say, the enforced medieval ghetto was for most of us Jews not centuries ago, but only yesterday, and my parents migrated from medievalism to the modern age. Moreover, our generation has lived through, as if it happened not yesterday but only this morning, both the Hitler experience and also the creation of the State of Israel. Dating from the first large-scale breakdown of ghettos in Europe, all this has been compressed into a period of scarcely more than a hundred years.

The 20th-century migrations are quite a different matter from those of the 19th. It is the difference between relatively leisurely migration and drastic upheaval. Two years after my father came to America around the turn of the century, he was able to send for my mother and my two older sisters. He left a place of economic distress and limitations, of hostility and persecution. This, though, was quite different from the abrupt, overnight and death-dealing events that began in the 1930's and then in a period of about fifteen years brought to us Jews the very greatest calamity in our long history. In briefest terms, Germany and central Europe are today virtually bereft of Jews; in eastern Europe the remaining Jews are subject to the antireligious indoctrination usual in communist states, and, now cut off from Jews of other lands, they may in time disappear. The largest Jewish community is that of the United States; the second largest is the isolated community of Russia; the State of Israel is third. The community in France underwent great losses at the hands of the Nazis; it has since been replenished through the immigration of Tunisian and Algerian Jews, who are culturally French. The British community is somewhat like the American.

To repeat, the migrations of us Jews, whether in the 19th century or even in the 20th, have often involved a movement from closed communities into relatively open ones, and this latter is the case even in Israel, for Israel is in very many respects kindred to a Western state.

The effects of moving, as my parents did, from a completely closed ghetto community into a relatively open situation such as exists in the United States, do not become manifest all at once or in all aspects of living. The first thing which goes in such migrations is the old language, to be replaced by the language of the land. The cuisine and the family customs do not seem to need cultivation but quite naturally tend to continue. The religion, deliberately preserved, tends to abide, though it may undergo various forms of subtle or intentional alterations, and even though individuals may abandon it, and leave the Jewish community. But, to revert again to the word "recency": our Jewish experience, whether in moving from European closed communities to Western open ones, or whether confronting us with the need to assess the relationship of us Western Jews to the State of Israel, is so new, and involves as yet any unfinished processes, that the transitional nature of the changes implies that it is premature to make final appraisals. That applies too to a Jewish attitude to Christians.

Christianity in Transition

You Christians are in your own way also involved in an uncompleted process, and again the word "recency" finds its relevancy. In western Europe in the 16th century you split into two segments, Catholicism and Protestantism, and your Protestants became even more fragmented, especially in the ensuing centuries. You fought your various religious wars, and practiced your persecutions of each other; then in the 18th century you began to learn to live with each other, though in varying degrees of warmth or coolness.

In the 17th century new trends in "humanism" foreshadowed the decline of the "medieval Christian state," and in the 18th century it began to disappear and the "secular" state began to emerge. Moreover, the 18th century gave birth to a new spirit which challenged much of the past, whether the divine right of kings, or the validity of your religious assumptions (and, by implication, ours). Deism and biblical criticism began to make inroads in your traditions, and only the ghetto walls spared us Jews at that time, for they kept these things away from us. There still abided in the Christian population the distinctions implied by peasants and nobility, or slaves and slaveowners, and you Christians yourselves did not all possess uniformly those rights which a free citizen can expect to have today, and which the modern state is expected to furnish and protect.

In modern secular states, church and state became legally separated, or even where they did not, the state church became increasingly of less vital significance in government policy, and this change has affected you in various ways, especially in the matter of the free conscience versus religious authority.

In the 19th century you found yourselves further divided, beyond mere denominations, because of your different responses to the implications of the new, modern age and the new, secular culture. Some of you wanted to preserve your traditional Christian beliefs from the effects of the new sciences and the new history, by seeking to insulate your tradition from them. Others of you preferred to try to blend together the new learning with your ancient beliefs. Accordingly, you became divided on the issue of how much, if any, of the new age you would absorb. By and large, the Catholics among you made the attempt in the 19th century to reject modern science and (for brevity let me say) modern "culture," as exemplified in the celebrated *Syllabus of Errors* of Pope Pius IX in 1864. The Protestants among you, in different decades, split into "modernists" or "liberals," and "conservatives" or "fundamentalists"; often this Protestant division was urban versus rural, or the schooled versus the unschooled. In the meantime, certain of your Christian traditional concerns, such as education and charity, began to become the responsibility and the prerogative of the state, thereby depriving you of some portion of the way your churches used to serve your people, and this development contributed to reducing the retention of your full interest and even loyalty to your religion. The more that science and education flourished, and the continuing industrial revolution brought about shifts of population from the rural areas to the cities, the more there grew among many of your people an indifference to religion. Many of you remained Christian only in a loose, formal way, and large numbers of you abandoned even the loose affiliation. Within your churches you engaged in all earnestness in doctrinal quarrels, as over evolution, and heresy trials, these not completely outlived, as now exemplified in the matter of Bishop James A. Pike. Often the public-at-large was either amusedly curious or else quite indifferent about these things. Since your divisions set you against each other, your divisiveness increased the general apathy.

It has been only in the past decades that many of you have come to recognize the somewhat uncertain, perhaps even perilous state in which your religion stands in the Western world. (Some of you still do not recognize this.) It was among you Protestants that there arose the impulse, called "ecumenism," to rise above your divisiveness and pool your strength; ecumenism has come to include Catholics since Pope John XXIII and, indeed, the strongest impulse in ecumenism is today probably theirs. There abides, among conservative or fundamentalist Protestants, a continuing dissent, or opposition to, the ecumenical trend; rather curiously, the spectacular growth in your denominations in recent decades has been in the fundamentalist sects which often oppose ecumenism, and not in the liberal Protestant churches which have embraced it.

Your theology has traversed movements such as "rational liberalism," "the social gospel," "neo-orthodoxy," "demythologizing," and even the "death of God." Eminent names in the 19th century challenged your right to exist, such as Nietzsche and Feuerbach. Marx spoke of religion, meaning Christianity, as an opiate (he hated too the Judaism which his parents had left to embrace your faith), and Darwin outraged many of you by his theory of evolution, and Freud provided a basis on which some of you have been willing to transform sin into mental illness.

The separation of church and state ensued after the many centuries of their union in both Catholic and Protestant lands. The Western world is today religiously a patchwork of anomalies, with separation prevalent in some lands, a national Protestant church found in some countries, and the Catholic Church still the official religion in other states. Yet even in those countries where the legal separation has taken place, large and irregular vestiges have held on. For example, divorce is prohibited in some countries by the civil law; a Christian holy day, Christmas, is a legal holiday in the United

States; and the public schools, even when church and state are ostensibly separated, are in many ways geared to a Christian, Protestant civilization, and understandably retain many mementos of the time when the Protestants were, without challenge, the sole religious force in a Western country. In a sense you are still involved in a transition in its own way quite as drastic as ours, and a final judgment on where you will come out is also premature.

The Encounter with Each Other

We encounter each other today in the midst of these transitions. In the past few years you Christians have issued public pronouncements about us and these give us some idea of your attitude, composite as it is, toward us. I provide some of these below, pp. 90-95. All in all, these are friendly, and a reversal of the past. Hence, reasonably, you have seemed to wonder about our attitude to you. If I sense this right, you seek for something more detailed, perhaps more profound than what your Jewish next-door neighbor or your Jewish business associate may be able to provide.

It is only we Jews in the free West who feel a certain urgency to express an attitude to you. Yet such an expression does not seem likely to emerge from any of our organized groups, primarily because we Jews have almost uniformly abstained from corporate pronouncements of a religious character. Moreover, there does not exist among us any counterpart of the Vatican Council, nor any single encompassing organization of all of us Jews. We have many types of organizations, but not any one authoritative organization. In the complete absence of a pronouncement by any corporate body of us, a statement can come only if one person succeeds in devising a formulation which may be able to gain the assent of his fellow Jews. I am cognizant that my formulation may fail to win such assent. In any case, I feel that a statement should at last be made, if only to serve as a point of departure for further focusing of thought, and a more adequate expression, subsequently, by others.

Christian versus Gentile

I must, moreover, quickly move to an assumption which influences these pages. While some of us Jews use the terms "Gentile" and "Christian" interchangeably, I do not. By Gentile, I will mean the dictionary definition, namely, a Gentile is a person who is not a Jew. This definition tells us more in the negative sense, about what the person is not, than it does about what the person is. A Christian is a Gentile, and so is a Moslem, and so is a Buddhist. While, therefore, a Christian is a Gentile, a Gentile is not necessarily a Christian. I shall mean by Christian a person who shares in some minimum ways in Christian beliefs, is likely to belong to a particular Christian church and to participate in its settled devotions, and who would consciously describe himself as a Christian. You Christians are apt to be just as aware as I am, or probably even more so, that in our time many so-called Christians are so only in a sentimental sense, or have been born to Christian parents, while themselves neither possessing Christian convictions nor affiliating themselves with some church. Indeed, in our time, the word "Christian" has come to be a synonym for a decent, or kindly, or ethical person; it has become a frequent experience among us Jews for one of us to be described admiringly as the "finest Christian" in the town, or in the university, or in the army division. I will have to take some account of the situation, for which there is a distinct Jewish parallel, of Christians who are so only through origin, and not through active convictions or formal church membership.

The Past and Today

Though I deliberately address myself to the situation today, you and I can understand it only by some reference to the past. Can one understand American Negroes without remembering slavery, the Civil War, the Reconstruction period, the segregation epoch, the social and economic problems? Yet my intention is by no means to present still another rewriting of what has been called "the Christian-Jewish tragedy," but only to use the past to make the present all the more clear, so that the meaning of "recency" and "transition" can be understood. Space in a small book is at a premium; I shall restrict myself to that which in the history was usual and dominant—and will refrain from noting all the unimportant exceptions.

The need for a book such as this arises from the history of our relationships with each other. Once these relations were completely negative, both collectively and individually; we are grateful that a change has been achieved. What have we learned, and can we learn, that can make our relations to each other the most affirmative?

3

SOME ASPECTS OF HISTORY

The Parting of the Ways

Your religion was born within ours. Jesus and his disciples were Jews. For a relatively short period of time, your religion was a Judaism, one of the several varieties that existed within the Judaisms of that time. In those days, Palestine—or Judea, as it was then called—was a Roman possession; Jews, though, lived throughout the Roman empire, but especially in the eastern Mediterranean where the Greek culture, of what we call the "Hellenistic period," continued to dominate. Indeed, there were more Jews outside Palestine than in it.

Within a few years after the belief in the resurrection of Jesus arose to give your beginning movement a new and strong impetus, the fledgling "church" spread beyond the borders of Palestine. It welcomed Gentiles into itself, and in the matter of a few decades the movement outside Palestine consisted largely of people once Gentile. Palestinian Jewish Christianity played so small a part in the unfolding of the movement that we today are largely in the dark about it, and the few scattered items we know are not clear or certain. At the time immediately after the belief in the resurrection arose, the "church" was guided, perhaps ruled, from Jerusalem; soon new centers arose: Antioch, Damascus, Alexandria, and Rome; not much later the Jerusalem leadership disappeared, though just when the transfer of leadership to other centers took place is not known to us.

But since your religion was born within ours, and either left ours or was pushed out—we do not know which; probably a little of both—you and we share some things in common. We are also distinguished from each other by some striking differences, which will need to be described. But first, we must notice respecting today that in addition to the differences to be listed, there exists a significant lack of balancing factors. For example, since your religion was born within ours, you faced the need to define your relationship to us in a way in which we have not felt the need to do toward you. You had to find some way in which to assert your belief that you were a continuation of the Judaism of the Jewish Bible; you have named it "Old Testament," and you seldom speak of it as the "Jewish Bible," since you regard it as fully a part of your own. Next, you have needed to explain, primarily to yourselves, in what way you have believed, and often still do, that you supplanted us in God's favor, and you have needed to account for the changes you introduced into the Judaism which produced you, and for the additions you made which went beyond the changes. Much of your earliest literature deals with these topics. The Gospels contain a great amount of material which presents Jesus as simultaneously a loyal Jew and critical of his fellow Jews; and they portray him as founding the new religious entity, Christianity.[1] The Epistles, especially of Paul, deal with Judaism rather than with Jews; they set forth the bases on which Paul advocated an approach to the ancestral Judaism that was drastically different from the approach of both ancient and modern Judaism. Paul held that the laws not only did not bring their observer to righteousness but were, indeed, an obstacle to it, and therefore were null and void, and that the proper way to righteousness was through "faith."

To put this in a quite different way, Paul's argument is that your altered version of our common ancestral religion is the right version, and ours wrong, while the argument in the Gospels is more often that we Jews are wrong people while you Christians are right people. Some of the other New Testament literature deals with the quite different problems you had with the Romans. There were also problems that you had with each other,

[1] Your scholars disagree about this last statement, for some assert that Jesus himself did not found the new entity, but remained within Judaism. The word "Christianity" arose (Acts 11:26) well after the new movement was launched, and until the word arose you probably considered yourself simply to be Jews.

for you quickly became divided into approved opinions (that is, orthodoxy) and disapproved opinions (heresy) and you could be, and were, most bitter to each other.

An important lack of balance to which I must point exists in the Scriptures. Your Christian Bible, in the part that is the New Testament, mentions us Jews by name, and it asperses both us and our Judaism. Our Bible, your Old Testament, since it dates from a time previous to the rise of your religion, naturally contains no mention of you, and we Jews cannot turn to it for direct guidance about you, as you can turn to yours about us. Our Bible is scarcely charitable to ancient peoples such as the Canaanites and Edomites, and if these had chanced to survive to our day, then we Jews would need to ask ourselves if we can subscribe to the attitudes there expressed. (We like it that our ancient rabbis tell us the quaint anecdote that when the Egyptians were drowning in the Red Sea, and the Israelites proceeded to sing the triumphant song recorded in Exodus 15, God rebuked them: "My children are drowning—how can you sing!") We Jews figure as villains, all of us or some of us, in much of your Bible. Only very lately has this bothered you extensively and intensively, and the reality has to be faced that some of you are not bothered by this at all. Your sacred literature is just as harsh on your fellow Christians who were "heretics" as it is on us; but the heretics who lived at the time when that literature was written disappeared from history, as did the Canaanites and Edomites, whereas we Jews have survived.

Your Dominance

Another lack of balance is the obvious one that you have been numerous and we few. In Europe we lived in the midst of a civilization in which your religion grew to the point of becoming the official religion of the Roman empire. Once you attained that status, you took steps to root out all the other extant religions; it is likely, though not fully certain, that we Jews represent the descendants of Jews who came into Europe after your triumph, and that Jews who were there earlier were driven out or absorbed. You spread beyond the Roman empire throughout Europe. We did too, in small numbers. In your view, we Jews represented a wrong people with a wrong religion, and you were therefore reluctant to let us find a place of dignity in your civilization. Both church law, enforced by the state, and state law prompted by the church, excluded us from the normal gainful pursuits by which people earn a livelihood, and you devised ingenious kinds of restrictions, such as making us wear a "Jew badge" to identify us, and you persecuted us most cruelly and unpityingly, and you expelled us, broken in body and spirit, from domain after domain. In different ages and in various localities, you tried the device of compulsory conversion, and then found yourselves astonished that these turned out to be perfunctory and insincere. You became all the more infuriated that we did not abandon our religion and turn to yours. The lack of balance in these matters is that you were in control and we were subject to your power.

There are other lacks of balance. For example, there arose among you a spate of writings, outside of and later than the New Testament, with the sole purpose of denouncing us; these were usually called "Against the Jews." If we produced such literature about you, it has somehow failed to survive to our day. When it turned out to your 13th-century inquirers that a handful of passages in the ancient rabbinic literature either disparaged you or else seemed to you to do so, you used the power of the state to burn our books, or at least to expunge the passages distasteful to you. Tragically, you allowed yourselves to believe slanders and lies about us by Jews who converted to Christianity, and you rewarded these converts with material gain. In those days there existed no free contest in an open arena for the possession of the hearts, minds, and loyalties of men, for by your laws those of us who converted one of you were subject to death, as was the convert.

All the above is very brief. When the details are filled in, they will sound to your modern, Western ears as incredible as they do to ours, and you can still be shocked by what Hitler did, but possibly not be surprised. If we are to try to understand the context of these medieval occurrences, we need to remind ourselves of the terrible cruelty of the times. For example, in the year 1096 during the First Crusade, the Jews in the Rhine valley of Germany were almost entirely wiped out, either economically or physically; in the Fourth Crusade in

1202-1204, the Western Christians sacked the Eastern Christian capital of Constantinople. The Fourth Lateran Council of 1215, when Innocent III was pope, issued a number of decrees against Jews; it was this same Innocent III who stimulated the "crusade" against the Albigensian heretics of southern France, as a result of which these Christians were exterminated. It was the law in many Christian states, England for example, that a Christian heretic, on conviction by a church court, was to be turned over to the state for burning at the stake (*De Haeretico Comburendo*). The law remained in force in some European countries into the 18th century. "Witches" were burned in Europe and America in some abundance.

Your Treatment of Us

To the modern age, some of those medieval incidents and attitudes are fantastic to the point of a joint unwillingness, yours and ours, to credit that they took place, for this happened not under an insane Hitler, and not against the dominant spirit of an age, but under presumably sane people, and yet fully in keeping with the spirit of that age. Foremost among the astonishing medieval occurrences was the "blood accusation," the Christian charge that we Jews require the use of Christian blood for ritual purposes, and to obtain it, commit assault and murder, usually on a child. The first recorded instance comes from the 12th century.[2] The best-known

[2] A somewhat comparable allegation arose in pagan Egypt in the

medieval instance is that of Little St. Hugh of Lincoln, best known because Chaucer mentions it in the beginning of his "Prioress' Tale." Jews were forced to stand trial on such charges, and were tortured into confessing, and normally both the perpetrator and the community he represented were then sentenced to death. Just in the past months, the Vatican has put an end to the observance in Trent, Italy, of the "martyrdom" of Blessed Little Simon who allegedly was murdered for his blood by Jews in 1475; this ending came about as a result of an inquiry into the surviving documents made by a Catholic priest, Father Willihad Paul Eckert. The recorded instances throughout Europe of the blood libel number into the hundreds. The justice of my use of the word "medieval" can be questioned, as intimated above, for this sort of thing has persisted virtually into our own days; recently, in 1966, two books, Bernard Malamud's *The Fixer* (fiction) and Maurice Samuel's *Blood Accusation* (nonfiction), have dealt with this accusation in Czarist Russia in 1911-1913, an accusation ("the Beiliss affair") which resulted in an actual trial and a reluctant acquittal. Such incidents occurred in considerable numbers even in the enlightened 19th century, and even though previously Christian scholars, especially Cardinal Ganganelli (1763), had repeatedly demonstrated the absurdity of the charge, and popes, beginning

1st century. The Book of Exodus celebrates a Hebrew triumph over Pharaoh and the Egyptians. The large Jewish community of Jews in Egypt had translated the Pentateuch into Greek. Egyptian pagans read Exodus, or heard about it, and, quite naturally, responded to the ancient disparagement with a contemporary one.

with Innocent IV in 1247, had repeatedly condemned it.

You were not immune from superstition (any more than we were). There developed among some of you a tendency to identify us with the devil, or at least to credit us with demonic powers, against which you felt the need to protect yourselves. Often you accomplished such self-protection through the seemingly demonic possession of portions of the Christian populace, with the result that, even against the teachings of your religion about love and against the counsel of your leaders, there were those of you who embarked on the pillage and murder of Jews and the destruction of Jewish communities, desisting from neither mayhem nor rape. The word *pogrom* is Russian; it means desolation or devastation; it has made its way into English dictionaries as meaning an organized massacre of Jews. It is a 19th- and 20th-century word, for in eastern Europe the pogroms abided long enough to be vivid recollections of Jews living today. The recollection is still vivid in my own family, for my oldest sister remembers the pogrom from her youth, and I, born in the United States, vaguely recall various anecdotes about fire and flight and concealment which I heard from my parents who fled to America from pogroms.

It is not my intention to consume page after page with a recapitulation of the well-known horrors through which we Jews lived at the hands of you Christians. I should make it clear that there were those among you Christians in almost every age and country who tried valiantly to spare us; a number of popes took measures to protect us Jews within the limited rights given us. In general, the higher the rank of the clergyman, the less he was associated with the spontaneous disorders (though he could be part of the planned ones); the lower the clergyman, the more apt he was to be associated, and in all too many cases he became the instigator. For our purposes it will suffice to summarize: You developed, almost from your beginning, theological judgments on us as people and our religion, and these judgments were totally unfavorable. Through church or state law, you limited us economically and politically; you tried through seduction or coercion to convert us; you persecuted us in a variety of ingenious ways; you confined us to dwell within ghettos, closing our communities off from the general culture of the age, and from your noblest people. Can you understand sympathetically that you, collectively, have tended to forget these things, but that we tend to remember them?

Your Repudiation of Religious Bigotry

I recognize that there are many of you, especially in the Western hemisphere, who have never laid a finger against us or spoken an unseemly word about us. Can you not say therefore that I am making too strong a summary? The answer is that I am not. If anything, I am restraining my pen. But the occasion for this book is not that you Christians have persecuted us, but rather that you Christians have in such numbers turned against this persecution. You have broadly dissociated yourselves from it, you have denounced it, and often in the past century you have come to our assistance. Out of these changed circumstances, almost reversing nearly two thousand years of history, have come your recent declarations about us.

4

THE FASHIONING OF ATTITUDES

I must digress to raise an important question, whether I, in the light of my being a specialist in New Testament, a serious student of Christianity, and thereby or therefore apparently *persona grata* in Christian circles, have had so exceptional an experience as to be disqualified from a balanced appraisal of you Christians. Am I too partial to you, as a reviewer charged respecting my *We Jews and Jesus*? My personal objective is neither to magnify Christianity nor to belittle it, but only to understand it and to portray it accurately in my teaching, speaking, and writing. My obligation as a scholar is not to Judaism but to the truth. One never quite succeeds in attaining full objectivity, but one constantly strives to. I have been concerned about how to couch the truth I have wanted to speak, for I see no advantage in ugly writing, but the question of how to couch a matter has always been secondary to me compared with the substance I have essayed to interpret. As to my Jewish loyalties, the titles of some of my books proclaim my identification; I have never considered that identification to be a franchise for deliberately incorrect statements.

Yet statements about you, made from my vantage point, would be for some differently situated Jews—my east European grandfather, for instance—so far removed from their experience that they would seem to be incorrect statements. My grandfather, who never came to America and whom I never knew, was permitted to encounter the cruel among you, the unlettered, the uncouth, the rapist, the murderer; his in his time was the typical Jewish experience with Christians. I, on the other hand, have known your scholars, many of your leaders, many of your clergymen, your students, in almost invariably cordial and congenial circumstances. My grandfather was never privileged to know about the constructive and admirable achievements of your tradition, about your scholars, your devout mystics, about your eminent theologians, about your men of kindliness, and your ideal of love. Jews in his environment were wont to contrast the sobriety of us Jews with the drunkenness of you Christians, for we seldom met the sober among you. On another level, a biblical verse, Genesis 27:22, "the voice is the voice of Jacob, but the hands are the hands of Esau," became a commonplace contrast between Jewish reasonableness and tolerance, the voice, and Christian intolerance and violence, the hands of Esau. Among us American Jews newer judgments now vie with this older view; the older view, however, still persists among some of us. The decisive factor is usually personal experience. I have taught in one of your seminaries, and lectured in others, and spoken to Christian assemblies too numerous to tabulate. I was trained in New Testament by great Christian scholars and great men; I correspond with a good many of them, and periodically meet with them at scholarly gatherings. Some of them are, to borrow a phrase, my best friends, and truly close ones. Thus my grandfather's judgment of you, and mine would necessarily be no less than antithetical.[1]

Such relationships, and the communication out of which they grew, would never have been possible for my grandfather, who was one of a people with almost no rights.

We Jews and Human Rights

Let us trace some of the process by which we Jews moved from a people with almost no rights to a changed status where we were granted rights. There has existed for us Jews in the past two hundred years the experience of various sad outcomes to an understandable wish on our part for those elementary human rights that spur all sensitive men. In western Europe

[1] It concerns me a little that the nature of this book necessarily brings into focus an overwhelming array of negative matters, and obstructs a reflection of the genuine respect that I feel for so much of Christian achievement, which I have written about elsewhere.

the physical ghetto walls began to fall in the 18th century. In that remarkable age of enlightenment, certain 17th-century developments' entailing partial religious toleration, were carried further, and thereafter became a quite general principle accepted in many Western states. In the 17th century in England, for example, Milton in his *Areopagitica* and John Locke in his *Letter concerning Toleration* argued for religious toleration, that is, that the state should abstain from interfering in religious matters, having in mind here the differences among you Christians. The Act of 1689 in Britain granted freedom of worship to dissenters, but not to Roman Catholics or Unitarians. Such 18th-century thinkers as Rousseau and Voltaire in France, and Lessing in Germany advocated universal tolerance. Lessing's play, *Nathan the Wise* (1779), embodied in his plea for tolerance the figure of a Jew, Nathan, who was benevolent and generous; that play is an important milestone in the history of the acceptance of Jews in the Western world, for it was of tremendous pioneering significance, especially since in earlier drama the Jew was a deep-dyed villain, as in Marlowe and Shakespeare. The 18th-century tolerance came to be part of the American Bill of Rights, and of the French Rights of Man. This tolerance was initially not that by Christians of Jews, but by Christians of each other; where it came to be extended to Jews, this was usually only coincidental. Normally, you Christians constituted an articulate and powerful obstacle to our achieving our goal of freedom and equality. Where we achieved it was not thanks to you, but, quite candidly, despite you. Accordingly, in very many parts of Europe, the older discriminations abided virtually unchanged, so that in most countries we Jews usually lacked the rights of citizenship, the right freely to earn a living, and the right to be educated. We lacked, of course, the right to hold public office; the final disabilities in this latter were not removed in England until 1858. In 1809 a Jew, Jacob Henry, had been elected to the North Carolina legislature, and his right to be there was challenged on the basis that he was not a Christian.

In our Jewish history books, this wish for citizenship in the past two hundred years goes under the name of "emancipation." Emancipation was achieved in the United States without a struggle, and in Britain with only a limited one. Emancipation implies the acquiring of *rights*, and not simply the benefits of mere toleration: "We hold these truths to be self-evident, that all men are created equal, and they are endowed by their creator with certain inalienable rights." This American belief animates us Jews, both respecting ourselves and respecting all men.

It is a fact of Jewish experience, however, that such legal rights, which the government can and normally does protect, are often quite distinct from the opportunity for the pursuit of happiness which society, as distinct from government, controls or shapes. We see this vividly today in the situation of Negroes; we can say in the United States (except for certain local situations in some laggard parts of the country) that the legal rights of Negroes have indeed been established, but their pursuit of happiness has been approved and abetted by only part of our society, and is impeded by a larger portion, even in the North. Moreover, even in the parts of the country where the collective society seems to have the disposition to make that pursuit of happiness readily available, factors such as poor education, poor housing, and poor preparation for advantageous employment constitute problems which yield to ultimate solution but do not yield to immediate ones. On the one hand, one understands most sympathetically the heightened impatience of Negroes, and on the other hand one recognizes the tangled knots which seem to require time for untying, even if good will were limitless. Whereas all too often governments lag behind society, and make legal the changes that society has endorsed, in many areas society lags far behind the government. This is glaringly the case with American Negroes. It has been the case in the United States of immigrating groups, such as Irish Catholics in the first half of the 19th century, and Italian and Slavic groups in the 20th. Such, too, has been the case of us Jews. One might put it in this way, that the American government has been essentially neutral on religion, and, though necessarily indifferent to Judaism, it has been hospitable to Jews as individuals; on the other hand, American society, largely Christian, and pre-eminently Protestant, has harbored varying measures of hostility, both consciously and unconsciously. Thus, a Jew could have the right to vote and to attend the state university, but could be barred from admission to a resort hotel or a social club, or the medical school of a private university. The government, being neutral and secular, affirmed our rights; society, largely Christian, preserved disabilities. Two hundred years ago you opposed us and hindered us. Then in large measure you changed. This situation today is indeed vastly improved over what it was a generation ago (as in the 1920's), and that was vastly better than two generations ago. But there has been bred in us American Jews a mixed attitude, in which the recognition that we had inalienable rights was blended with our recognition that we continued to face the struggle for the pursuit of happiness. A problem often before us, respecting the pursuit of happiness, has been whether you Christians as Christians would help us or hinder us in that pursuit. To this matter I will return.

The "Christian" State

In Europe, except possibly for Britain, Holland, and Scandinavia, the situation was somewhat different from America. Emancipation in central and eastern Europe was elusive, and the effort to achieve it was abortive; as one moved eastward, it was increasingly futile. In the early 19th century there was added to the age-old difficulties of Jews in Europe a newer conception associated with the beginning of the rise of nationalism. (We need to recall that in the 18th century there was no single entity Germany, but only a large aggregate of kingdoms, principalities, dukedoms, and free cities, welded together by Prussia between 1866 and 1870;

similarly, prior to 1870 there was no single entity Italy.) The beginning theories of nationalism first conceived of the state as a *Christian* affair, with the implication that there could be no room in the Christian state for a Jew. In various parts of Germany, before and just after Napoleon, whose fall increased the many diverse nationalist sentiments, the emancipation of Jews had made slow progress, only to undergo setback and reversal. But in the ensuing decades, the more nationalism grew, the less prospect there was of Jewish emancipation. After the liberal revolutions of 1848 failed in various parts of Europe, emancipation was even more remote from achievement than it had been in 1800. In German lands, the road whereby an individual Jew could become a lawyer, or a doctor, or a public official remained that of conversion to Christianity, with the result that eminent men, such as Heinrich Heine, typically went through the formality, Heine so as to be admitted to a law school. Such conversion was scarcely a matter of conviction, but the Christians were willing to accept the formality as if it represented authenticity. A Jew, aspiring to an education or a career, faced the issue, as did Heine, of whether or not he was willing to go through with conversion so as to achieve his goal.

The "Racial" State

The developing nationalism then underwent a further alteration. Certain theorists ceased to conceive of proper nationals in terms of language or religion or political inclination, and began in a preliminary way to conceive of nationalism as a matter of *race*. Some 19th-century writers set forth absurd views not only about race in general, but about the qualities, admirable or despicable, which are supposed to inhere in the races. These definitions, especially in the decline of Christian influence in Europe, assumed that only a Gentile was a proper national, and that someone of Jewish birth or ancestry, even if he had become a Christian, was not eligible. The exclusions of us Jews prior to 1800 were essentially religious; the new theories justified these older exclusions on the new basis of "race." Such racial pretension was prominent even in France, which witnessed a number of anti-Jewish outbursts in the 19th century, especially after the defeat in war by Prussia in 1870. An upshot of this French trend was the arrest, trial, conviction, and condemnation of Captain Alfred Dreyfus on the charge of having furnished military secrets to the Germans. The complicated Dreyfus Affair (1894-1906) involved a union of Catholic clerics and royalists against the French Republic wherein church and state had become separated.

Ultimately Dreyfus was vindicated as innocent. Yet how much rested on the guilt or innocence of one man! The fate of Jews in Europe at that time seemed to depend on the integrity, or lack of it, of one solitary individual. Suppose, for example, that Dreyfus had been guilty, and had confessed to guilt; is it reasonable that the fate of a people should rest on the innocence or guilt of one person?

The Failure of Emancipation in Europe

Most of us Jews who lived east of Germany had come to believe, out of the 19th-century nationalistic developments, that there was no realistic prospect for Jewish emancipation in Europe. An age-old Jewish theological doctrine held that God, through the Messiah destined some day to come, would lead us Jews from "exile" and back to Palestine, miraculously. This hope came to be influenced by European nationalism, with the consequence that a kind of imitative Jewish nationalism arose. It is called Zionism. Its essential basis was religious, with authentic roots in the Jewish tradition; its newer contours now became nationalistic. In the mid-19th century, Zionism, then in its early stages, was to be found primarily in eastern Europe, where emancipation had not advanced far enough to encounter setbacks such as took place in Germany in the 1840's. At the end of the 19th century the Dreyfus Affair, arising in free, enlightened France, brought Zionism into western Europe. (At that time, the bulk of articulate American Jews, content in their American emancipation, opposed Zionism as a defeatist rejection of the spirit of freedom of the wondrous age of the 19th century!)

Racism

The Hitler attitudes toward us in the 20th century grew out of the 19th-century theories of nationalism and race. It had been assumed that Jews were

"Semites," that is, a "racial" group. Previously, and correctly, Semitic referred to a group of related languages, not people, and it was recognized that, with the tremendous conquests by ancient empires and the migrations and intermingling of peoples, various peoples could adopt and exchange languages. In this newer and absurd view, "Semite" and "Aryan" became terms for peoples instead of for languages. In this light, the ongoing unfavorable attitudes toward Jews came to be known, illogically, as "anti-Semitism," and this absurd term has come to be too well established to be uprooted. The centuries-old Christian hatred of Jews provided a ready-made basis on which racial nonsense could be erected. A hundred years before Hitler, a Jew could escape disabilities by conversion to Christianity; under Hitler a person—even if he were a Catholic priest—with one Jewish grandparent was defined as a Jew, and could not escape. And the death chambers awaited him.

It should be clear that the Hitler persecutions were not religious as such, but quasi-racial. Though the previous religious basis made Hitler's anti-Semitism possible, there was the indirect result that Hitlerism, in expressing theories of Aryan supremacy, turned out to be anti-Christian too; in principle Hitlerism repudiated Christianity as a detestable "Jewish weakness," able to corrupt the true strength of pure Aryans. One might even go so far as to say that Hitlerism persecuted Christianity, though not Christians. On the other hand, the Vatican made a treaty, a Concordat, with Hitler, on July 20, 1933; the German people were uniformly Christians, and the churches in Germany, with only minor exceptions, either agreed with or at least conformed to Hitlerism.[2] A German Jew, either driven from his country or sent to his death in a concentration camp, could scarcely be expected to discern between the racialism or the Christianity of his persecutor, for these blended together all too well.[3] The Nazis as persecutors did what Christians had often done before, except that the Nazis worked their cruelty with infinitely greater efficiency and relentlessness. European Jews were shocked by Hitler; American Jews were shocked, and also somewhat surprised, for we scarcely expected such things to come out of so civilized a country as Germany. And we American Jews had come to have favorable relations on a quite extensive scale with American Christians.

American Anti-Jewish Movements

What kept us American Jews from being entirely surprised was the noticeable quantity of Hitlerism which appeared in the United States in the 1930's. True, we had legal rights; but society preserved discriminations. Now active agitation against us was arising even in the United States! For us it was a trauma to hear on a coast-to-coast radio network, week after week, a Catholic

[2] See Arthur C. Cochrane, *The Church's Confession under Hitler* (Philadelphia, 1962).

[3] On the other hand, the Danes, just as much Christian as the Germans, protected and even saved the Danish Jews, this through a dramatically executed transporting of them from Nazi-dominated Denmark to free Sweden.

priest, Father Charles Coughlin, tell vicious lies about us and do his best to stir up the American populace against us. Possessing only hunch and no knowledge about the inner workings of the Catholic Church, we were astonished that the Church permitted him to do these things, and we tended to the conclusion that he did so not only with permission but also with active sanction; after all, we had undergone very frequent persecutions at the hands of Catholics in Europe, and there was the Concordat between the Vatican and Hitler. Other anti-Jewish movements of that time were almost invariably led, not by secular maniacs, but by Protestant ministers, representing, as it were, obscure or tiny fringe churches, the names of which most of us had never heard. Your Christian leaders disowned these bigots. But you can understand that we Jews nevertheless could not dissociate all Christians from being a source of fear and anxiety to us. A few of us held a view, and still hold it (to my regret) that none of you is completely free of potential danger to us.

The Altered Modern Scene

World War II wrought many changes. The peoples who fought Nazi Germany tended to take those steps to purge themselves of Nazilike sentiments, and indoctrination in democracy proclaimed anew the equality of mankind. War service brought into the armies, navies, and air forces young men from all kinds of backgrounds: Mayflower descendants, first-generation Italian Catholics, Swedish Lutherans, and Jews, who lived and fought side by side. The military chaplaincy brought rabbis, priests, and ministers into common situations, into cooperative endeavors, and into warm personal relations. Immediately after the war, most private universities decreased or eliminated the abominable quotas on Jews, and welcomed a sort of counterpart to the university Y.M.C.A., the Hillel Foundation, to the campus (I served in this way at the University of North Carolina prior to the war and at Yale after it, with my office in the Y.M.C.A.). Professorships, previously withheld from us Jews in the United States, opened up in increasing numbers. Indeed, in very large measure, Protestant Christianity in the United States often turned out to be a notable source of support to us, and the discriminations which were persisting were those of secular American society, consisting of Christians but no longer representing organized or authentic Christianity. At that time the peculiar reserve in the Catholic Church, and its chosen isolation, impeded such association of our rabbis with Catholic clergymen as they had with Protestants, but at that time the distance between Protestant and Catholic was quite as great as that between Catholic priests and rabbis. But Jews and Catholics who were not clergy had learned through the war and the postwar changes to know each other better. In a word, even in the 18th century Christianity was our enemy; in the 19th century this began to change and you came to our assistance on a number of occasions when sharp persecutions of us arose, as in Damascus,

Syria, in the 1840's and the pogroms in Russia in the 1880's and in 1903; in the 20th century we Jews and you Christians, especially you Protestants, found the beginning of a new spirit existing between us. Since Pope John XXIII this new spirit has come not only to include you Catholics, but you Catholics have often taken the commendable initiative to overcome the past. In the 20th century we Jews and you Christians, despite Hitler and also because of him, have managed to forge some bonds of union in utter contradiction of almost 1,800 years of experience.

But society changes slowly, and there abide in it vestiges which are sometimes matters of genuine disability and sometimes matters only of unchanged usage, irritating nuisances rather than disabilities. Respecting the former, even today some fields of employment, or progress upward, remain closed to us Jews, and some Jewish doctors still find hospital privileges closed or restricted.

But so significantly have matters changed for the better that in the United States at least we stand on the threshold of understanding each other. It is to this understanding that this book is dedicated. But some ignorance still exists on both sides, and sensitivities persist; mystification seems to manage to hold on and irrational animosities, frighteningly, still persist. In our time, in the same half century in which a third of us Jews died at Hitler's hands, and in which some of us Jews fashioned the State of Israel, we American and British and Dutch Jews have found a deepening sense of solidarity with you Christians. Let me say it again, that this is all very recent and all very much still in transition.

Strains and Tensions

There is a variety of situations in which, and levels on which, we meet together. We come together usually in cities, not in rural areas, for we Jews are largely an urban group, and many of you from small towns have never met any of us (and often have strange notions about us, as if we in some way are markedly different from other human beings). In cities, our wives and yours encounter each other at the grocery store, or at a PTA meeting, in contexts devoid of Jewish or Christian significance. Our men and yours can belong to the same luncheon club, or serve on the same civic committee. At other times, civic enterprises often are fashioned through religious congregations even for enterprises which are not essentially Jewish or Christian, and committees can be formed with Jews and Christians serving as representatives of congregations. Nationally, there are occasions when your organized denominations and ours have reason to meet together through representatives. Again, there are times when a bill is pending before Congress and individuals representing this or that group or organization may testify before a Congressional committee; sometimes, as was the case respecting civil rights, Jews and Christians by and large espoused a common viewpoint, whereas respecting church and state, Jews often differ with Christians, and, indeed, Christians with each other.

In most of these contexts, which seldom involve a level of social intercourse but, rather, a matter of "business," a friendly attitude generally prevails except regarding church and state relations, where the attitude can become devoid of friendliness.

You must try to understand one facet of us Jews of today. Shylock said, "Sufferance is the badge of all our tribe." "Suffer" in Shakespeare's time meant "permit," and the time has passed for this concept. To be permitted by others is quite different from having rights within oneself.

The theme of self-emancipation which arose in Europe—that we Jews must primarily rely on ourselves—permeates many of us Jews. It means that we insist on right, not on permission. Respecting the Arab world and its complicated situation, the tragedy prevails that the ordinary relations between Arabs and Jews in the past were quite different from those between Jews and Christians, for often, indeed usually, Jews in Arab lands found hospitality, encouragement, and opportunity; and the current hostility in the Middle East is of very recent origin, the result of the clash between Zionism (and the resultant State of Israel) and the Arab nationalism that has arisen in the past half century. Respecting the State of Israel, we Jews (except for those of us totally opposed to the State of Israel) rest our contention on our "rights"; the Arabs, of course, deny these "rights," and assert their own.

The implication of "rights" and of self-emancipation and self-reliance finds its echo also among us Dispersion Jews. Where we Jews have obtained the rights of citizenship, we have insisted that the rights be full rights, not partial. Moreover, we emphasize that *rights* imply a possession which one is entitled to, and not a restricted set of privileges that can be conferred, whether grudgingly or wholeheartedly, by one person or one group to another. Often what might bring you and us together abstains from touching on rights as such, but there are times when this matter has some bearing. Accordingly, we feel that we are justified, in relationship to various types of controversial public issues, to exercise those full rights, especially respecting some limitations and to us distasteful practices from which society has not yet completely purged itself.

There are suppositions which linger on into our age quite naturally from the premodern period when church and state were united, so that church-state relationships provide a checkerboard of anomalies. Quite naturally there continue to exist both assumptions and practices which strike some of us as not yet in alignment with that neutrality which a Western state should observe, especially where church and state are separate. In American public schools, the period from Thanksgiving to Christmas is host to work units focused on Christmas, such as the singing of carols or a stage performance of Dickens' *A Christmas Carol.* Also until recently, the practice prevailed in schools of opening the school day with prayer, often a Christian prayer, or a Bible reading, often from the New Testament. Moreover, there exist in various areas systems of parochial schools primarily, but by no means exclusively, Roman Catholic (there are such Jewish schools too), and both a desire and an economic necessity have prompted representatives of parochial systems to advocate government support for these schools.

On the one hand, there are those among us, on the principle of exercising our free rights, who oppose in an absolute fashion any concession that the state might make to a religious community or even to religion.[4] Often this attitude among us aligns us with opponents of religion and even with atheists, and we are frequently in direct opposition to some earnest Christian groups. A few years ago a Catholic publication, *America,* commented that our opposition to federal aid to education was arousing anti-Jewish sentiments, and another Catholic publication, *Commonweal,* rebuked *America,* interpreting that comment as a threat which implied that the price we Jews might pay for our stand

[4] My personal position is not the absolute one held by many Jews. Believing, on the one hand, that the state should be neutral respecting the practice of religion, I do not consider it inconsistent for public education to provide instruction in the academic disciplines and the historic literatures of religion. The issue to my mind is where and how; that is, the public universities certainly should, the high schools possibly, and the grammar schools should not. The instruction should be academic, and free of denominational control (and bias). The instructors should be designated for their competency, and not as representatives of denominations. The state should bear the cost, since the offerings are academic; I find it most uncongenial that some universities solicit Jews for funds to support a chair in Jewish studies, but use general funds for chairs in Christianity.

was an increased anti-Semitism. A dilemma constantly before us Jews is whether we shall choose to give up the right as free citizens to take whatever stand conscience prompts in us, or instead to stand by our rights, even though the result could be the possibility of a reprisal by society. When the matter is put this way, the inevitable election must be to stand by our rights.

Yet there are many among us who suggest that strategy and tactics are as important as the goal of rights, and they therefore counsel that the realities demand a certain prudence, a certain restraint. Such counsel, so it seems to me, arises from two related but different considerations. The first can be put in this way: In the American context there has arisen a desirable situation in which the three great religious traditions, Catholicism, Protestantism, and Judaism (note that the Eastern Orthodox Church has usually been left improperly unnumbered and omitted), constitute the great spiritual resources of the country, and they have developed patterns of amicable cooperation, which, it is argued, ought not be disturbed, for they give promise of an ultimate solution to divisive issues. Accordingly, interreligious understanding is more important than for Jews to win some individual point in one of the controversial issues, as, for example, the eliminating of Christmas units in the public schools.

The second consideration is more complicated. It can be called the Jewish appeal to the Christian. This appeal has nothing to do with any desire or effort to convert Christians to Judaism. Rather, it amounts to soliciting

Christian sympathy and assistance on behalf of our Jewish plights and our Jewish causes. The origin of this is to be traced to the occasions in the 19th century, especially in the West, when Christian leaders spoke out or lent their assistance on behalf of Jews in response to acute moments of the persecution of us Jews. Once, then, where you had been as it were our enemy, you became in actuality our friend, and beyond that actuality you were potentially a very good friend. In this sense your Christian good will to us Jews, especially in an era of horrendous fright such as occasioned by Hitler, has naturally seemed to many of us Jews as a resource we have needed urgently to have. Moreover, Christendom represents organized and influential segments of citizens (local churches are to be found everywhere, and are near at hand to turn to), whereas the "secular" bearers of good will, though they are frequent, are sporadic, indistinct, and, in this sense, hard to appeal to. Aware of this area for recourse, there arose among some of us Jews a quite spontaneous, unpremeditated impulse to seek you out, as a small people will do, even when it believes in self-emancipation. Sometimes this approach has been single, individual, unorganized; sometimes it has become organizational, as for example in the National Conference of Christians and Jews and its counterparts across the Atlantic.

This approach to you Christians has been either a plea for assistance, such as enlisting your favor for a pro-Zionist attitude in the Christian-Palestine Commission, or suggestions for cooperation, as in "Institutes on Judaism for Christian Clergy," in local synagogues, or in pulpit exchanges, or in scholarship funds for Christians to study Judaism, or quite simply, the extending of favor, as in Jewish awards to this or that Christian dignitary for his "humanitarianism." (Recently the American Jewish Committee made awards to five Cardinals to thank them for their part in the approval by the Vatican Council of its Declaration on the Jews.)

In this matter of enlisting your support, we Jews are by implication petitioners, and almost all of us have some measure of disapproval for the particular form of petition that others of us resort to (I felt mortified at the award to the five Cardinals), for such forms strike one or another of us as lacking in that sense of dignity which is essential in any situation. To be blunt, I have the feeling that there have been some of us Jews who often have been no less than lickspittles in the petition to you Christians, and I suppose that other Jews have a comparable opinion of me. Only if you Christians bear in mind that, because there arose a Hitler, the stakes for us seem to us to be no less than that of our safety, in fact our lives, can you understand a sometimes groveling manner which some of you have said that you find irksome.

Anomalies exist by the score. For example, some of us Jews will invite one of your clergymen to give an address or invocation at some intra-Jewish affair, and then become offended when the Christian visitor uses his ordinary prayer form, ending with a mention of Jesus or the Christ. Some of you are alert to this sensitivity among us Jews, and seem disposed and able to offer a "neutral" prayer. Some of us Jews do not understand that in inviting you Christians, we need to assume that you will pray as you ordinarily pray, and that we Jews ought to abstain from inviting you unless we are prepared to hear the words you ordinarily use. On the other hand, I have been present when a Christian visitor has used the occasion, within his supposed prayer, to laud his faith, and indirectly, or even directly, to asperse ours. I once was introduced in what was intended, I am sure, as a highly laudatory way, as another Nathanael, "an Israelite without guile" (John 1:47)—though not in such a way as to suggest that all other Israelites are!

The only formula that I know of which should guide and shape our relations with each other, on whatever level, would presuppose self-respect, equality, and dignity. In a context of rights and our belief in self-emancipation, on the one hand, and society's limitations and defects, on the other, with you Christians a vital resource to appeal to, and with such continuing survivals as the forms of purely Christian culture that we feel are misplaced in our public schools (*misplaced,* not evil), we Jews have a delicate task as to how to proceed with respect to you Christians. If, on the one hand, I cannot agree with that tiny minority of my fellow Jews who scorn you and your religion and your help, I also cannot agree with an all too frequent, though unconscious, truckling to you. Moreover, I think that I know enough of you in enough intimacy to feel that overwhelmingly you do not want us to truckle. I think I know enough of you to conclude that one thing that you at your best do not want is for us to fear you. But even as one purports to stand on the words "self-respect," "equality," and "dignity," it is often a matter of opinion whether or not some particular venture has these or lacks these. I fear that the extant cooperative ventures have come too often at our initiation, not yours, and I feel that there needs to prevail an equality in this matter of initiation, and indeed in the participation in the projects, as well as in the substance of them. But is it not possible to separate the stand we or you may take on a public issue from the relations that you as an individual have with his Jewish neighbor? Can these stands be matters of impersonal principle, and not occasions for personal animosity?

We must not assume that we will have unbrokenly smooth relations with each other. Periodically extremists from both our communions will say or write extreme things. And we shall have occasion to differ in the character and the intensity of our respective responses to situations. An example of this prompts my adding to this book, the manuscript of which was completed in April 1967, the following comments in mid-July, respecting the Middle East war which erupted on June 5. For us Jews, the events of the preceding weeks were frightening. The Straits of Tiran had been closed to Israeli shipping; massed forces of the United Arab Republic had approached the borders of Israel; Nasser had demanded, and received, the withdrawal of United Nations forces;

and King Hussein of Jordan, previously an enemy of Nasser, was reported in the press, and seen on television, as joining with Nasser in the announced intention of destroying Israel and of driving its Jewish inhabitants into the sea. Our Jewish anxiety could scarcely have been greater, especially since Israel was the haven for refugees from Hitler's oppression. On the day hostilities erupted, the State Department announced that the United Nations was neutral in word, thought, and deed; later in the day "neutrality" was reinterpreted as different from unconcern. At the United Nations the Russian delegate used the most unrestrained language in denominating Israel as the "aggressor." In our Jewish anxiety, countless of us drew sustenance from the way, including tangible ways, in which Christian neighbors and friends expressed their solicitude.

Since antecedently we Jews and you Christians had cooperated on the national level in many enterprises, such as civil rights, many Jews assumed that the same outpouring of sympathy for the beleaguered Jews that animated next-door Christian neighbors would be reflected in the organized Christian bodies. Beyond this expectation, some Jews, in the acuteness of their anxiety, solicited support from Christian organizations, and even pressed for it, perhaps unduly. To the consternation of these Jews, such support was not forthcoming. While prominent Christian individuals spoke out in concern for the Jews in Israel—for example, Bishop Hallinan of Atlanta, President John C. Bennett of Union Theological Seminary, and Professor Robert McAfee Brown of Stanford University—the national Christian bodies assumed the attitude of "neutrality." *The Christian Century* in one editorial proclaimed its "neutrality," and in another (not in a news item, but *in an editorial*) printed a speech made, but not fully delivered, by a representative of the National Council of Churches of Christ; this speech, prepared for a hastily convened assembly of Jews held in Washington on June 9, was singularly inappropriate, and the National Council would have been better advised not to have sent a speaker to the assembly than to have been represented by such an address. The speech was interrupted and ended by the announcement of the cease-fire. It was scarcely the speech for that occasion, for the Jews assembled there could scarcely have responded warmly to the exposition of the Council's "neutrality."

This Christian neutrality has seemed to be based on the premise that at stake in the Middle East is only a political issue, a matter of the claims and counterclaims of rival states. For us Jews, on the other hand, our partisan concern was humane, our anxiety about our fellow Jews whose extermination had been publicly promised. In the dismay at the Christian neutrality, some Jews felt completely abandoned by precisely those Christians with whom they had had so much affirmative cooperation, and there were those who said bitter things. Indeed, some Christians, not at all neutral, wrote to newspapers letters as venomous about Israel as the words of the Russian delegate to the United Nations, and wrote these letters *as Christians.*

There are among us Jews those who infer from the above events that Jews need to be reconciled to going it alone, and to regard Christians as no real resource of help. Others among us have contended that in the decade in which the Vatican Council and various Protestant bodies have disavowed anti-Semitism, with the result that it is not respectable for a Christian to be an open and articulate anti-Semite, the historic Christian anti-Semitism has been judiciously channeled into the extreme and unjust hostility to the State of Israel. Some Christians have explained the silence and neutrality as of this kind: they have opposed American involvement in Vietnam, and they consistently opposed a possible involvement in the Middle East, for a consequence of such an unpopular involvement would have meant the emergence of pronounced anti-Semitism in the United States. Some Jews are inclined to view the matter as only a most unfortunate misunderstanding, resulting from the failure of adequate previous mutual understanding, in that neither Jews nor Christians had fully understood each other's premises regarding Israel, and hence the disparity between the interpretation by Jews of their concern as humane, philanthropic, and the neutrality of Christians, stemming from their seeing the matter strictly as Middle East politics. But still other Jews have wondered that those very Christians who were silent in the portentous days of threat, and neutral when war erupted, have not hesitated to express a concern about the holy places, and presume to demand the internationalization of Jerusalem now that the cease-fire is more or less in operation.

On the day that the war erupted, I was personally oppressed almost to the point of paralysis by the fear that before the day was over, hundreds of thousands of Jews would be slaughtered. I expected Israeli valor, but scarcely a military victory. I am personally not a nationalist, for I hold that all nationalisms, Israeli or Arab, or American or Swedish, contain a potential for great evil; I believe in world government. I have personally always regretted the absence in the past twenty years of any signal instance of some expression by Israel of concern for the Arab refugees, for its unconcern has seemed to me to match the unconcern of the Arab states, since the latter have seemed to me more interested in preserving a propaganda tool than in helping to solve a human problem. I personally felt let down by the attitude of the national Christian bodies, and by *The Christian Century*, even though I knew antecedently that since Christianity lacks the counterpart of Jewish "nationalism," Christians have often either failed to understand or else have been intuitively hostile to the idea of a Jewish state. Also, I have wondered passingly how the neutral Christians would have felt if Israel had been defeated instead of being victorious, and if the two million Jews there had been annihilated.

No, we will not have unbrokenly smooth relations with each other. Individual extremists will offend; the vested interests of national bodies, yours and ours, will from time to time move from legitimate difference of opinion into self-concern and into the exclusion of sound judgment and of basic humanitarianism. Yet what extremists say, or what national organizations, Jewish and Christian, do, ought not to be allowed to disturb the personal relations of Jewish and Christian neighbors.

Is Our Encounter Religious or Sociological?

I envy you Christians, and now especially you Roman Catholics, for the freedom you feel in airing your criticism of your practices and attitudes. We Jews do not feel the same freedom. Not only do we give special emphasis to abstaining from "washing dirty linen in public," but there are those among us who are quick to pin the label of "self-hatred" on any of us who trespasses into this area.

The sad fact is that there are some of us Jews who are marked by self-hatred. This is sometimes on the level of pure silliness; a cartoon I have seen depicts two Jewish women at a Christian worship service, with one whispering to the other, "If only we Jews had Psalm XXIII as part of our Judaism!" Sometimes it is the response to a drive for social eminence; in the context in which you Christians and we Jews maintain separate establishments such as country clubs, there are some of us who would prefer entrance into yours as more prestigious than remaining within ours. Hence there are among us those whom others of us call "*goy*[5] chasers." Sometimes self-hatred is the result of economic disability or the fear of it, as when a Jew sees, or thinks he sees, that his advancement in some large industrial firm is destined to be limited, not because of intrinsic abilities but by accident of birth. It is normal for a person to hate that which disqualifies him, and there are therefore Jews who hate being Jewish and hate Judaism. Such people would gladly leave us, if only they could. Often they can, but Hitler's definition of a Jew, namely, a person who has one Jewish grandparent, tends to close off escape from the Jewish community. Moreover, it is easier for a Jew to leave the Jewish community than it is for him to enter the Christian social community. It is easier to join a Christian church than to be admitted to a Gentile social club, and very often the former does not lead to the latter, as many ex-Jews have learned.

One of the consequences of the frequent migrations of the past century has been the tendency of an immigrant group (any group) to cluster in an area in a kind of self-imposed ghetto. We Jews have done the same thing; indeed, where we are numerous, we constitute a number of such clustered areas, dependent on the income factor—some of our youngsters speak disparagingly of our upper-income Jewish clustering as the "gilded ghetto"—and entered into depending on the

[5] *Goy* means Gentile. The plural is *goyim.*

presence or absence of restrictions which are social rather than legal.

This Jewish tendency (never totally observed) to live near each other combines with outside pressures and restrictions to effect a very anomalous situation. Free as might be our contact with each other in the daytime, in business and other ventures, we have relatively little contact with each other once night falls. A normal American city of any size harbors town and country clubs, both Gentile and Jewish; our colleges, and more tragically our high schools, harbor Jewish and Gentile fraternities and sororities.

I have the impression that these two separate communities are not quite so cut off from each other today as they were a generation ago. Certainly there is now freer association in business and in such public enterprises as philanthropy, the art museum, and the symphony. It is contended by some analysts that in two areas, namely, the world of arts and letters and the world of the college professor, these social barriers have almost entirely disappeared. Yet some Jews have told me of being dinner guests in a Gentile home at which all the guests on the particular occasion were Jews, as if the host inclined toward Jewish and non-Jewish dinner parties. In our "gilded ghettos," the affluent among us duplicate the luxuries found in comparable income groups among Gentiles. It appears to me that there is not an exact identity of this social situation in city after city, but only an approximate one, with the consequence that the exclusions prevalent in one city may not exist in another. I think I can take it as correct, however, that by and large we Jews and you Christians generally do not mingle with each other socially after six o'clock. Indeed, I suspect that whatever social mingling does take place is largest among the very young, decreases among our youth, and disappears among our adults.

We Jews are a middle-class, urban community. Factors behind us give us a vocational distribution which is slowly adjusting to the Western world but is still not identical. A great many of us are in retail trades, and our stores dot Main Street. Some of you never weigh the meaning of this visibility in relation to the huge, Gentile businesses like steel mills or automobile works which are not on Main Street and attribute to us a relative wealth which I wish we had, but don't! Social researchers continue to report that we Jews are excluded from certain occupations, or from advancement in "big business." We are comfortably off in the United States, and some of us are rich, but not in the way that the Fords, Rockefellers, and Gettys among you are rich. The facts about us are available in a good many "demographic" studies.

All these factors enhance sensitivities and suspicions. Perhaps you Christians have never felt the humiliation of having a reservation at a resort turned down because it did not take Jews. Perhaps you have never been asked by your high school children why two sets of social organizations exist. Have you ever looked at a home that you were interested in buying, only to learn that you would be unwelcome in the neighborhood, or that the realtor had some sort of understanding that he would not sell to one of your kind? Have you ever had your rise in your business career checked just below the executive level?

But, beyond the sensitivities and suspicions there arises the question of whether such experiences are inescapably what Jews must expect from so-called Christians. All this is very remote from theology, but it nevertheless impinges upon the attitudes fashioned by Jews, even in open societies, toward Christian people. These collective judgments are inevitably grossly unfair to individuals.

That is to say, much of the relationship between you Christians and us Jews is sociological rather than theological. All too often when some of us meet with you, your interest is in discussing theology, while our interest is human relations. Often those of us who meet with you are much more qualified in sociology than in theology, and on more than one occasion some of you have been a little mystified at what seems to you the lack of a Jewish religious interest on the part of those Jews who sit down to discuss common problems of religion with you. You find some of us not only devoid of religious knowledge, but even of a religious interest, at least in the sense in which you have a Christian religious interest; you seem to want to discuss topics such as redemption and salvation and messianism, and we seem to want to discuss economic and social problems. The reason is not that we Jews lack religion, or are exempt from religious problems, but that the concerns which are the most immediate and pressing to us deal with the mundane matters of our acceptability or even our safety. Moreover, we differ from each other not only in theology, but in our respective approaches to our different religions.

5

DIMENSIONS OF RELIGIOUS DIFFERENCE

Creedal and Noncreedal Religions

Your tradition contains creeds—short statements of what you essentially believe—and you recite these creeds in your worship services. While our tradition is marked by distinctive beliefs, these do not take on a creedal character; we have one well-known "creed,"[1] that of Maimonides, but it is one man's summation of the essentials of Judaism and not an obligatory prescription decided on by a convened body of authoritative persons. In your tradition *belief* was prescribed,

[1] It is found in the Orthodox prayer book in the daily service. The thirteen items can be summarized as follows: (1) God is the sole creator; (2) God is a unity; (3) God is incorporeal and is free from matter and form; (4) God is eternal; (5) God is the sole legitimate object of man's prayer; (6) the prophets are true; (7) Moses is supreme among the prophets; (8) Scripture as possessed is unchanged from that given to Moses; (9) the Torah is unchanged and cannot be superseded; (10) God is omniscient; (11) God rewards the faithful and punishes the unfaithful; (12) the Messiah, though he tarries, will come; (13) the resurrection of the dead will take place.

and your theologians have dealt with the various divisions and subdivisions of that belief, thereby clarifying its meaning and import; our theologians have dealt preeminently with obligatory obedient *conduct*, in its various divisions and subdivisions, and have largely ignored the definition and the clarification of the beliefs themselves. This statement holds true even though we Jews do possess some quantity of medieval Scholastic philosophy which is kindred to your Scholastic philosophy: the statement is true in the sense that the usual Jew is reared in practices and observances, such as holiday or dietary rules, and ethical injunctions, but not in even elementary theology. You Christians, on the other hand, deal with God, the Christ, the nature of man, the import of sin, and the like. If a neutral observer were to ask one of you what he believes, he would answer in terms of creed or theology, while one of us, if asked, would answer in terms of our Jewish sacred days and our ethical precepts. In a word, in your tradition, faith is explicit, and conduct usually left undefined or only implicit; in our tradition faith is left implicit and the conduct made definite and explicit.

The rise of secular humanism constituted a challenge to some or all of your traditional beliefs, including your inherited view of the Bible; for us the same movement, toppling the ghetto walls, created the problem of how readily possible it was for Jews on entering an open society to maintain the ancestral customs which presuppose something of a closed society. In the great upheavals in the Reformation era among you, while there were attendant circumstances of political and economic affairs, the religious issue was the dominant one, resulting in a division among you as to whether salvation lies in the church, that is, in the institution, or instead, in the Bible. Religious reformation among us was much, much less profound, for it dealt with issues such as altering the length of the services, and whether to retain them entirely in Hebrew or translate some or all of them, and what traditional usages seemed still viable and still necessary. For us Orthodoxy is the full range of *practice*, Reform Judaism a reduced quantity, and Conservative Judaism less than Orthodoxy but more than Reform; the theological differences are secondary, and were historically a second stage, not the first. We have almost no figures in our history such as Augustine, John Hus, Luther, or Calvin; such theological phrases as "justification by faith" and "predestination," and "the total depravity of man" are entirely outside our direct orbit. To go a step further, our tradition has lacked the structure and authority which the Catholics among you have inherited in the Catholic Church. On the other hand, the Bible was never as directly central among us Jews as it is among those of you who are Protestants, for the Bible for us is mediated through the rabbinic interpretation of it.

In such senses, our approach to belief is significantly different from your approach. Very few of us Jews are academically prepared to discuss our Jewish beliefs in the same way that many of you Christians are; and when you and we begin to discuss beliefs with each other, we often manage more to mystify each other than to enlighten.

But beyond this matter which I have called approach, there is a resulting difference, that you possess a sense of fervor about your beliefs, since these are crucial for you, while matters of belief among us take on the character of academic questions. You feel the obligation of believing, while our reduced obligation in this respect is often interpreted, or misinterpreted, as merely that of knowing. Some of your Protestant denominations were split into two on the issue of fundamentalism versus modernism relating to the divine origin of the Bible; our splits have never been on such issues, though such issues arose after the splits occurred. Can you imagine one of you who is simultaneously a Roman Catholic and a Unitarian? Among us, insofar as synagogue affiliation is concerned, a good many American Jews maintain active membership simultaneously in Orthodox and Reform congregations. If you comment that this latter seems fraught with inconsistency and even contradiction, then from your perspective you are exactly right, but we Jews have seldom been deeply oppressed by such considerations.

Significant Differences

One could go on and list other divergencies. For example, in your tradition the church is the key institution and the home subsidiary; for us the home is the key institution and the synagogue subsidiary. You tend to weigh fellow Christians on the basis of belief, with affiliation quite secondary; we weigh fellow Jews on affiliation and participation, with belief secondary. Sometimes we both fall into the error of weighing each other by one's own suppositions, so that some of us quickly conclude that your interest is in theological hair-splitting on irrelevant topics (shades of your Erasmus!), and some of you conclude that our interest is in the peripheral concerns of religion, not the central ones. Some of you, penetrating a bit into us, are dismayed that we seem very mute on topics such as God's election, the covenant, and the like.

Sometimes you find it a little hard to accept that among us the doctrine of the Messiah does not occupy the central place that it does among you. You wonder, too, that not only do we not regard Jesus as the Messiah, but that we seem relatively indifferent to the messianic views in our tradition. It is often very hard to persuade you that what you have meant by the Messiah is quite different from what we have meant, for your tradition greatly altered and amplified the conception you took over from us. If some, or even most, of you are bewildered that we Jews can abstain from "accepting" Jesus, an equal proportion among us is similarly bewildered that you "accept" him. The question of Jesus is a complicated one; I devoted to it the short book mentioned earlier, *We Jews and Jesus*. Let me say only this much here: when in the past you persecuted us in his name, we could scarcely be expected to honor and cherish that name. A schoolteacher once commented to me that Jewish students seemed to him to "cringe" at the mere mention of Jesus by name. In parts of Europe, many of us completely abstained from letting the name Jesus come to our lips. To you it has always been the supreme name among names; to us it was often the name through which terror arose among us. You must not be surprised that there hang on, among ordinary, random people in our midst, unreflective vestiges from the past. Yet, with persecution diminished, a good many of us Jews have written appreciatively about Jesus, though invariably about a man, a Jew, and not about the divine Christ of your Christian tradition. Your basic Christian suppositions provide a place for Jesus which our basic Jewish presuppositions do not; Jesus serves in your tradition in a role which does not at all exist in ours.

But let me move on to try to sketch in a broad outline of these fundamental religious divergencies between us. We have in common the Old Testament. It begins with the Five Books of Moses. For us, the central part of the Five Books of Moses is the laws, described there as divinely revealed, which begin with the Ten Commandments in Exodus 20. What comes before, especially in Genesis, namely, the creation, the flood, Abraham, Isaac, and Jacob, and the enslavement and release in Egypt, constitutes materials which edify us or inspire us by motivating us to emulate personalities whose achievements we celebrate, such as Abraham or Moses. But the nub of our religion is to be obedient to the divinely revealed commandments which begin in Exodus 20. These provide us with our ceremonies and, beyond them, with our ethics. In a way somewhat comparable to your appending the New Testament to the Old, we have appended to our Scripture what we call rabbinic literature, in which is achieved the extended application and interpretation of the laws, ceremonial and ethical, to diverse and multiplying situations. (The chief rabbinic literature is the Talmud, a two-stage compilation, written after first being oral, consisting of the Mishnah, recorded about A.D.[2] 175, and the Gemara, about A.D. 450-500; and the Midrash, a verse-by-verse interpretation of the biblical intent.) The point to notice is that though the literature of edification, such as the Psalms, abided among us, and our medieval scholastics produced religious philosophy, yet obedience to divine commandments has towered over these things among us.

You may remember that in A.D. 70, the Temple in Jerusalem was destroyed, and it has never been rebuilt. In the Five Books of Moses, the building of that Temple was enjoined, and it was to be presided over by hereditary priests (the Hebrew word for priest, *cohen*, yields the frequent Jewish name Cohen, and its variant spellings: Cohn, Kohn, Kahn). Jews had spread throughout the settled world long before 70; they had taken the Bible with them, and, where necessary, translated it, as into Greek in 250 B.C., and they had created an institution where they assembled to study Scripture,

[2] You Christians use A.D., "Year of our Lord," whereas many Jews insist on using C.E., "Christian Era."

to which among Greek-speaking people the Greek word "synagogue" became attached. Since the study of a sacred book tends to become similar to prayer, the synagogue has been both a school and a prayerhouse; the instructor in Bible was the rabbi, which means "my teacher." When the Temple was destroyed by the Romans in 70, synagogue and rabbi were already on the scene to substitute for Temple and priest; moreover, organized, systematic schedules of prayer replaced the scheduled system of sacrificing animals which had prevailed at the Temple (and which have been entirely missing from us since the year 70). The rabbi was not a priest, but essentially a teacher and interpreter of the Bible, and a lawyer or judge in the developing and broadening legal-ethical system. The Jewish view about obedience to law can be put in this way: Deliberate disobedience amounts to challenging God, and is unforgivable, and in time God, not man, will punish such effrontery. Accidental, unwilled disobedience is forgivable, and divine forgiveness can be sought by man through repentance and through man's atonement; moreover, a man possesses the capacity to repent and to atone, and the free will to choose whether or not to conform to the laws, and then to do so.

You will recall, of course, that Paul had taught that the laws, which, to repeat, begin in Exodus 20, were not the truly appropriate way to live the righteous life, for, on the one hand, a man was incapable of choosing to observe them; instead, he found the laws prompting him to disobedience, and, on the other hand, the laws were a second-grade revelation, not comparable to the substance found in Genesis about creation, Adam and Eve, and the patriarchs, especially Abraham. Paul taught that the laws were no longer in force, and that the righteous life was to be attained through man's complete submission of himself to God. Paul called this complete submission "faith," and he found in Abraham, who, of course, lived before Moses, the supreme example of the man who through complete submission to God achieved righteousness without needing the laws which came at the later time of Moses. (About a century after Paul's time, the explanation arose that Paul had "abrogated" only the ceremonial laws, not the ethical ones.) The consequence of subordinating the laws to the contents of Genesis was a shift from the centrality of laws, as such, to biblical "history." It involved a shift away from the Jewish assumption, something everywhere else unchallenged in Jewish writings, that a man could choose to observe the laws and succeed in doing so. Christianity challenged the assumption that a man could choose to observe the laws or could carry out his choice. Whereas for us Jews the laws, as in Exodus, were central, for Christianity the "history" of mankind in Genesis supplanted that centrality of the laws.

Thus Christianity came to a different view of man from that which we Jews had, and have. Specifically, Christianity held that Adam, the forefather of all humanity, who sinned in Eden, transmitted to all his descendants the guilt for his trespass. Hence, sin (and evil) is inherent in all men, and as a result, a man is by nature unable, alone and unaided, to rise above sin. Abraham rose above sin, through his total submission to God, and God graciously reckoned Abraham's "faith" as righteousness; it is God alone who can redeem man from sin. The coming of the Christ was God's way of providing mankind's redemption from Adam's sin, for when the Christ died on the cross, that death was an "atonement" for man's sinful nature, available to all men who had "faith," that is, who submitted themselves completely to God. Thus, while Jews held that a man could by his deeds achieve religious rightness, Christians, especially those to whom Paul had been the guiding voice, have held that it is only the grace of God which can bring man to his rightness. To the Christian, the man who has not experienced the supernatural grace of God remains unredeemed; the career of the Christ Jesus is held to have brought salvation to previously unredeemed man. To the Jew, man was never lost in sin, and hence not in need of salvation in this sense. This is what I meant by the statement that in Judaism there is no such role for Jesus which exists, as it were, for the Christ in Christianity.

But to proceed with the contrast implied above, of the centrality for Jews of laws originating in the Bible, and the emphasis on salvation-history to the Christians, each tradition possessed the divergent approaches, already in the first Christian century, and then went on to develop them, quite separately of course, and always in increasingly divergent ways. Jews embroidered the laws, Christians embroidered the history of salvation;

Jews continued to attribute to man the obligation to observe the laws which were progressively expanded and refined, firm in the belief that man could do so, or else could repent if he slipped. You Christians raised questions about the nature of man, and about which men—surely not all of them!—would receive divine grace, and you supplied the answer that supernatural grace came to those individuals who were "predestined" for it. With the passing of time, you Christians probed these questions all the more deeply, raising issues such as whether man in any sense had any freedom of choice at all, or whether God's grace providentially either came into a man or abstained from doing so. You Christians did not agree with each other: Augustine (354-430) insisted that man can be "saved" only by the grace of God, and only those out of the mass of men whom God had elected to receive His unmerited mercy were saved; Pelagius, who lived in the same era, taught that man could on his own take the initial steps toward salvation, quite apart from grace, and moreover, if man was in no way responsible for either his good or evil deeds, the lack of responsibility implied that there was nothing to restrain man from indulgence in sin. The views of Augustine and Pelagius were antithetical, in that Pelagius assumed man had some choice, and Augustine, that man had none. Pelagius, however, was condemned as a heretic, and his opinions as heresies. I cite Augustine and Pelagius only in capsule illustration of the Christian probing into questions about the nature of man, of grace, of faith, the relevance of which is that such probing and such questions neither received comparable attention in Judaism nor resulted in the decision that some one view was orthodox and another heretical.

Judaism never produced creeds, that is, short, authoritative statements of obligatory beliefs; nor did it develop the inner organization out of which to proclaim with relative universality which view was orthodox and which heretical. Jews differed with each other on the meaning of laws, or on their application, but always in the context of ascribing authority to the law they were disagreeing on; they never issued proclamations on those elements in the religion which we may call theology or dogma; they restricted themselves to the elements we might call practice.

Among you Christians there have been protracted debates, and proclamations by church councils, on what the orthodox view about the nature of God and Jesus must be, and which views are heretical; even though much of this question of heresy or orthodoxy belongs to the past, you are nevertheless still capable of some division on the question. I do not think I exaggerate when I say that such metaphysical disputes among you are so far outside our ken as to be incomprehensible to us; equally incomprehensible to you are our disputes on tiny details in our practices. Indeed, the real situation between you and us about the metaphysical Christ is not even so deep as the difference of belief, for it scarcely goes that far; we simply do not understand you at this point, and you simply do not understand us.

And those who have tried to clarify this, through the device of oversimplifying, seem only to have made the obscure even more unclear.

Similarity in Ethics

I do not see any great difference between us in the matter of what we both regard as ethics. We differ in our formulations about ethics, and in the weight we give to it in our respective traditions. We Jews *never* divorce ethics from religion; your tradition, deeply committed to ethics as it is, nevertheless has often managed to set it below your advocacy of total submission to God, and some of you even tend to dissociate ethics, "works," from your Christianity. Our chief differences, however, are not in ethics, but in theology, and in our respective manners relative to theology.

Religious Usages

Yet alongside the theological differences I feel the necessity of adding an oft-omitted consideration that I regard as of possibly equal weight. Religions do not exist in vacuums, but are carried by people. A religion presumes a religious community. Religious communities develop ways of doing things, norms, and criteria, and usages, all of which can be remote from specific theological doctrines, and in some of these usages, which can constitute the warp and woof of a religion, we differ also. The celibacy of the Catholic priest is as strange to us as our Passover *seder* ("order"), a sacred meal, preceded by prayer and ultimately giving way to children's rhymes and the attendant humor, is to many of you. Your tradition has prohibited divorce, but by and large has come to tolerate it (except for those of you who are Catholics); our tradition has permitted it, but has uniformly discountenanced it. I believe that there is a broader, wider adulation of education among us than has existed or used to exist among you, and I do not intend by this an evaluation but only a description. In our tradition the highest rung in the social scale went to the man of learning, not to the man of wealth. We Jews scarcely know any limits to our partiality for education.[3] In our own time, it is reported that we Jews, constituting 3 per cent of the American population, constitute 10 per cent of American college students.

The ascetic tendency is more pronounced among you than among us. Monasticism is unknown to us and we felt no need to formulate, as did you Protestants, a doc-

[3] Recently, in a very ugly situation in Wayne, New Jersey, the Christian vice president of the Board of Education publicly and successfully opposed the election of two Jewish candidates on the charge that Jews are too generous, too liberal, and he implied that with them as board members, taxes would rise. What a vice!

The same person added an additional disqualification, that the election of these two Jews would contribute to the further elimination of Christ and Christianity from the public schools. This was, of course, an appeal to Christians to intensify the latent Christian anti-Semitism, and to make it as nearly overt as possible. I sometimes think, perhaps uncharitably, that those Christians who are willing to muddy the separation of church and state, this by means of concessions exclusively to Christianity, are attesting to the failings in Christian churches and homes to meet their responsibility for Christian education, and thereby imply that the public schools should make good the deficiencies.

trine of "vocation," that is, that men are "called" for a diversity of forms of religious achievement, though this view is quite essentially like our own unformulated assumption.

I believe that we Jews have been so shaped that we respond to philanthropy, in the sense of charity, in an unparalleled way. Philanthropy is a primary constituent of our religion, not an outgrowth of it. Our term for charity reflects a unique transformation in the meaning and enacting of a word. The biblical term, *tzedaka,* means righteousness. In our postbiblical literature, and in our use of the word even today, it is altered to become synonymous with charity. In the medieval ghetto we maintained orphanages, old-folks' shelters, funds for the sick, loan funds, outright support for the indigent, funds to provide dowries which in those days were the prerequisite for a poor girl if she was to marry, collections to maintain schools, and the like; indeed, we were prepared to make an emergency assembly of funds to ransom Jews either imprisoned by state authorities or seized by pirates. In the modern world in which philanthropy has become scientific, and perhaps too much so, I have known Jews to object to some procedures which have come about, but I have not known of, or heard of, any Jew who challenges the assumption that to be philanthropic is an essential mandate of our religion. Indeed, there are some Jews in our time who, finding no sense of personal relationship to the worship service in the synagogue, express their Judaism one-sidedly in philanthropy. Nothing in my experience or my reading leads me to conclude that your estimable Christian philanthropy is quite as central to the religion, or as markedly accentuated, as is our Jewish philanthropy among us.[4]

You can read explanations about Judaism and Christianity which contrast a supposedly this-world emphasis in Judaism and otherworldliness in Christianity. The key to a proper understanding here is to focus on the word "emphasis"; it is incorrect to contrast the Christian and Jewish attitudes totally. Themes of otherworldliness are found in the traditional Jewish writings, and Christian ethical responsibility has obviously dealt with this world. Furthermore, traditions as old as Judaism and Christianity have naturally harbored historical periods in which the themes of this-worldliness and otherworldliness, found in both traditions, have been heightened or lowered.

There has been a great decline in the West in the quantity of Jewish knowledge a Jew possesses. Your Jewish neighbor is scarcely apt to be so informed in Judaism as to be fully apprised of the long history of Jewish thought. Rather, he responds to general trends and general instruction in Judaism, as these are medi-

[4] I have heard it reported that some American Jews hostile to the nationalist ideology of Zionism, and therefore unwilling to contribute funds for Israel, have found an agreeable outlet for their Jewish philanthropic impulse in contributions to such worthy enterprises as the American Friends Service Committee! That is, the unwillingness to give to a particular purpose is overcome by the Jewish mandate to give. (One needs to notice, however, that universal as philanthropy or charity is among Jews, there are, unhappily, a small number who represent the margin of difference between most and all Jews.)

ated to him from his attendance at synagogue worship or a synagogue school, and not from exact knowledge. Accordingly, he may tell you, incorrectly, that Judaism never had a conception of hell, when the fact is that it did, and that you Christians took it over and greatly elaborated it; he knows, though, that by and large hell has disappeared from our usual Jewish thought. Your Jewish neighbor is quite unaware of the depiction of heaven in some of our Jewish writings; this representation is much less extensive and complicated than it appears in your tradition, and is, instead, a kind of vague, indistinct belief among us. Again our traditional prayer book is committed to a belief in resurrection, but we Jews have often inclined to interpret it as immortality, just as you Christians have; the Reform Jewish prayer book has substituted immortality for those passages which in the old prayer book read resurrection, and neither concept is specifically emphasized. While our tradition includes the belief that reward or punishment for good deeds or evil ones can await the individual after death, by and large these are not vivid matters to Jews, and, not entailing obligatory belief (for we have no creeds or dogmas as such), they are interpreted quite diversely by both informed or uninformed Jews, or are often more or less ignored.

Only in a small number of us will you find the theme of denying the physical pleasure of this world, but overwhelmingly we Jews subscribe to the view that this world is a place which we must enjoy. Vows of poverty and celibacy which characterize Catholic clergy are totally unknown to us. So, too, unknown to us are certain practices or views which prevail among some of you (or at least once prevailed). We have no religious objection to the use of liquor, but an objection only to drunkenness. We have not objected to the use of tobacco, nor have we ever espoused "plain dress," that is, a hat without a hatband, or a suit coat without lapels. Our tradition would prohibit us from being gourmands, but never gourmets (and that is why "kosher" delicatessens in very many places tend to become gourmet shops). "Kosher" means something in between "proper" and "clean," and strictly speaking should be applied only to food originating and prepared in such a way as to conform with ancient regulations; in this sense, meat can be kosher (that is, beef, lamb or goat, properly slaughtered, but not pork or shellfish), but dill pickles cannot be kosher. In our time kosher has come to be extended to certain foods which are merely the traditional cuisine of large segments of our people, but by no means to all of us. *Gefilte* fish (stuffed, spicy fish) or *kasha* (groats) are foods that some of our forebears brought to the United States with them, but these are quite unknown to others of us. The standard joke of comparing one's wife's cooking with one's mother's is probably no more than a reflection of a tendency among people to cherish the flavors of childhood food; hence, many of us incline to so-called Jewish food, but even this can so vary according to the region of origin of one's European ancestors that a wife's cooking can completely fail to resemble a mother-in-law's in any way! Traditionally we Jews have kept dairy and meat foods separate from each other, and similarly we have used different kitchen utensils and dining-room china for the two. Many Jews in our time have come to disregard the traditional regulations about food, either totally, or partly and inconsistently (for example, some Jews who would never dream of eating pork will assent to eating the equally forbidden shellfish); some Jews will run their household in complete fidelity to the traditional food laws, but ignore them, partly or entirely, outside the home. It should perhaps be stated clearly that since there has been no authority of persons in Judaism able to repeal traditional laws,[5] the food laws remain in force, as it were, and Jews who do not observe them have let them fall into disuse. If your Jewish neighbor strictly maintains the "kosher" practices, he can enjoy your home hospitality short of eating your food. If that is his bent, you Christians should never assume that he is rejecting you or your hospitality, and you should understand the implicit inequality in that he can feel free to serve his food to you in his home, but not eat your food in your home. There would be nothing amiss, if you have the impulse to entertain a Jewish visitor, to ask him, without embarrassment, whether or

[5] I do not here overlook the action of some assemblies of early Reform Jews which passed resolutions denying the binding authority of rabbinic expansions of scriptural laws. The meat and dairy distinction is rabbinic, not biblical. The point in context is that of the absence of authority in Judaism to repeal or abrogate, and hence I stress disuse rather than authorized alteration.

not you might serve him food, and he will not be embarrassed to give a genial and honest answer.

The divisions among us Jews (Orthodox, Conservative, and Reform), which highlight some of the differences just recorded, are not easily to be equated as identical to the divisions among you Christians. By and large your divisions are theological, and thereafter have resulted in differences in practice; for example, first Protestants denied the validity of intermediary priests, and asserted the "priesthood of all believers," and then proceeded to abolish the "confessional." With us the divisions arose in the realm of practice, and only thereafter became theological. Orthodox Judaism seeks to maintain the traditional ways indicated in Scripture, and spelled out in rabbinic literature, without change or reduction. Reform Judaism preferred to abbreviate the worship service, and to couch it in the language of the land rather than to maintain the traditional, universally Hebrew one, and to seat men and women together, rather than to keep them separate at worship, and to reduce the quantity of the inherited laws, and not to abolish laws (or customs) as such. By and large, Conservative Judaism is a reaction away from the alleged extremism of the reforms of the Reformers, and was designed to attempt to preserve a larger quantity, but not the totality, of the inherited practices. Only at a later stage did theological issues enter in, and by and large these were at first relatively peripheral (that is, they dealt with the personal Messiah and the return to

Palestine rather than with God or the Bible), and only later did they become more centrally theological. Your Jewish neighbor will be much more aware of the difference in practice (the seating of men and women together, the use or disuse of the skull cap, known as the *yarmulke*) than he will about theological issues. Moreover, these divisions among us, though often felt intensively by the pulpit, are treated with elasticity by the pew, especially in the United States, and these divisions scarcely ever impede a maximum cooperation and Jewish unity in matters of philanthropy or health and welfare. Synagogue affiliation bears some relationship to the size of the city and the community; in general, Jews in small cities almost unanimously maintain a formal affiliation, and bear the financial responsibility; the larger the city, the less encompassing is the synagogue affiliation. In the very large cities there are Jews who are active in various phases of the Jewish community, who may neither attend a synagogue nor even maintain a nominal "membership." (Among some of you Christians, "membership" connotes a sense of personal religious experience, and does not relate to enrollment in a list of the affiliates of a given church; with us Jews, membership is strictly a matter of enrollment.)

Among some of you Christians, in particular Roman Catholics, church attendance is obligatory; in our tradition, synagogue attendance was expected of males, even though such expectation fell short of obligation, and our women were welcomed but not usually expected to attend. In this context it must be mentioned again that with you the center of the religious life is the church, and the home supplementary; with us, the centrality is the home where much of our religion is practiced and taught through time-honored ceremonies such as lighting the Sabbath candles, and the synagogue is supplementary. (There are however all too many of us Jews who have confused the lack of obligation to attend the synagogue worship with a presumed sanction for non-attending.) Just as among your urban Protestants, attendance reaches high points at Christmas and Easter, so among us there are the high points at the Jewish New Year and Day of Atonement.

This parallel is symptomatic. Western open communities tend to effect a kind of unconscious uniformity even among the diverse elements. For example, the Protestant minister is not a priest, but a layman; so too the rabbi is a layman, not a priest. Yet the trends in our complex urban life tend increasingly to make ministers and rabbis act as if they were priests, and to make the congregations more nearly akin to audiences than to active participants. The tendency toward such uniformity goes on apace; however, it scarcely affects those matters which might be described as the tone and texture of the attitude of an individual to his tradition. What this means is that if you are a Christian, you must not assume that a Jew has the same sense of relationship to his Judaism as you have to your Christianity, and vice versa.

Jews and Christians approach their cohesiveness differently. A writer has pointed out that the collective feeling of Christians for each other is to be described by the word "fellowship," that of Jews by the word "kinship." Certainly our being fewer in number and our having, despite our inner diversities, a common history of persecution and of anxiety about persecution increase our sense of kinship, especially when the times are threatening. We Jews are quite capable of becoming seriously and even bitterly divided among us, but this divisiveness recedes or disappears when an external urgency compels it.

The Responses to "Modernism"

Jews and Christians also seem to approach and respond differently to the complex series of issues raised by the rise of modern secular thought, which coincided with the fall of the ghetto walls. You Christians have had to handle the problem of how you can maintain your traditional supernatural beliefs in the light of the emergence of an age which has so largely repudiated supernaturalism; our instinctive response has been the different question: How can we maintain in an open society those practices of ours which fitted so naturally into a closed society? Perhaps I might put it in this way, that in the light of your emphasis on theological consequences, you were confronted by theological issues when Darwinism appeared, and you had the problem before that of reconciling Galileo's teachings with church assumptions. We, on the other hand, have had very little difficulty in such matters (for even the traditional among us have not been bound to the literal wording of Scripture as most of you Protestants have been). Rather, we have been confronted by problems such as the ability to observe Saturday as the Sabbath in a social situation where it is not the day of rest, or how our children can attend a university in a small town which lacks a Jewish community and still be faithful to our food laws. The open community is hospitable (despite diminishing but continuing barriers) to us as individuals, but disruptive of our corporate traditional practices.

Lacking the decisive theological rigidity which has characterized many of you, we have had very little difficulty in embracing modern scientific theories, or modern learning, or modern literature or art. We are conditioned to find a distinction between the sacred and the secular of only minor significance, for we have viewed all facets of life as potentially sacred, and the sacred as permeating the secular. Lately some of your thinkers have, as it were, either discovered or rediscovered "secularism," and have been struggling to find some form of reconciliation or congruency of Christianity with it; this sort of thing is ancient with us, and to most of us no problem at all in a theoretical way.

Yet it is true that, theology aside, some Jews feel seriously threatened by the modern scenes, and attempt to maintain, either little changed or totally unchanged, the characteristics of the social configurations of the closed medieval ghetto. Perhaps this impulse might be clearer if I mention a segment of the Israeli population which is at odds with the rest of Israel in that it preserves the medieval dress, the medieval Jewish education, the medieval attitude to woman, all this in a national state which is as modern and Western as any modern state, and whose universities, the Hebrew University and Technion, are as scientifically advanced as any Western university. These traditionalists—some call them ultra-traditionalists, for even among the traditionalists a range of elasticity or else rigidity has come about—are not so much in protest against modern science as they are in protest against the possible dissolution of the corporate Jewish life. Hence, whereas many Israelis have discarded traditional habits, such as the maintenance of the traditional tonsure (with curled sideburns), and incline to some disregard of the strictness of Sabbath prohibitions of riding or smoking on that day, the ultra-traditionalists will make no concessions at all. It can be correctly contended that theological issues are inevitably at stake and bound up in these matters. My point, however, is that the theological facet remains implicit and in the background, while the issues of protective practice occupy the foreground. It is in such a light that you can perhaps understand why some Jewish thinkers have expressed a preference to the term which describes traditionalism as Orthopraxy rather than Orthodoxy. The latter word would imply unchanged belief; the former, unchanged practice.

Except for the ultra-traditionalists in Israel or in isolated localities in the West, Jews, whether they are Reform, Conservative, or Orthodox, feel completely at home in the modern scientific culture. Perhaps I should modify the last sentence so as to note that in the past two decades we Western Jews have adopted from your theologians a beginning theological interest, as a result of which we have been breeding a growing number of theologically minded younger men who confront us with theological issues more or less comparable to your own, including a Jewish "death of God." This new approach is a necessary afterthought, it seems to me, to the complete adjustment we Jews have made in the world of modern culture. Now that we find ourselves at home in it, we consider it necessary to inquire and understand where we have suddenly found ourselves. Nevertheless, if I were to put into a simple contrast the distinctive character of Christians and Jews respecting a particular common problem, the Christian tendency would be to ask, What shall we think about this? while the Jewish tendency would be to ask, What shall we do about this?

Accordingly, there are many significant fine points, which, unperceived, have kept us from readily understanding each other's religions. Our misunderstandings, paradoxically, have been increased by some common possessions which we each use differently. The divergent use of the Old Testament, whether the emphasis should be on the laws or history in it, is only a single example. Beyond this, you and we quote the Old Testament, but often interpret the same verse in contradictory ways, and then we become puzzled that disagreement increases instead of giving way to agreement. We have used so variously elements which we have in common that we have often been totally blind to our possession of common elements.

Even beyond the abstruse questions of theological differences, then, religious traditions take on a corporate shape and develop particular motifs, and these latter, as I have indicated, seem to me quite as significant in the distinctions between religions as the theological. A problem that remains to us is that we have each generally assumed that one of us is totally right and the other totally wrong. I will return to this matter, for it requires exposition and also candor, since it remains an ongoing problem.

6

A NEW CHAPTER IN OUR RELATIONS

Persecution at the hands of Christians (as distinct from the hands of unchristian Nazis) is virtually gone from our day, especially in Western countries. I mean active persecution, and not the occasionally recurring hostility.

Indeed, so much favorable communication, flawed though it has been, has gone on between leading Jews and Christians, on both the national and the international level, and in local communities, that we stand today, respecting each other, in a situation quite the opposite of the age of medieval persecutions. What Christians might have condoned in the Middle Ages has come to shock Christian leadership in our day. Moreover, virtually all Christian minds agree that to some extent, small or more probably large, Hitlerist racial anti-Semitism was built on a basis of Christian anti-

Semitism. As a consequence, there are on record some post-Hitler statements from respected Christian sources that need to be quoted, since they express important facets of your Christian attitude toward us Jews. Here is a statement by the Protestant World Council of Churches, made in two stages. The First Assembly meeting in Amsterdam, in 1948, declared:

> Before our churches can hope to fulfill the commission laid upon us by our Lord there are high barriers to be overcome. We speak here particularly of the barriers which we have too often helped to build and which we alone can remove.
>
> We must acknowledge in all humility that too often we have failed to manifest Christian love towards our Jewish neighbors, or even a resolute will for common social justice. We have failed to fight with all our strength the age-old disorder which anti-Semitism represents. The churches in the past have helped to foster an image of the Jews as the sole enemies of Christ, which has contributed to anti-Semitism in the secular world. In many lands virulent anti-Semitism still threatens and in other lands the Jews are subjected to many indignities.
>
> We call upon all the churches we represent to denounce anti-Semitism, no matter what its origin, as absolutely irreconcilable with the profession and practice of the Christian faith. Anti-Semitism is sin against God and man.
>
> Only as we give convincing evidence to our Jewish neighbors that we seek for them the common rights and dignities which God wills for His children, can we come to such meeting with them as would make it possible to share with them the best which God has given us in Christ.

The last sentence is an allusion to the Christian wish to convert the Jews; here let me only note the allusion, for later I must discuss this matter.

At its Third Assembly (New Delhi, 1961), the World Council adopted an additional resolution. It begins by hearkening back to the Amsterdam resolution, and then proceeds:

> The Assembly renews this plea in view of the fact that situations continue to exist in which the Jews are subject to discrimination and even persecution. The Assembly urges its member churches to do all in their power to resist every form of anti-Semitism. In Christian teaching the historic events which led to the Crucifixion should not be so presented as to fasten upon the Jewish people today the responsibilities which belong to our corporate humanity and not to one race or community. Jews were the first to accept Jesus and Jews are not the only ones who do not yet recognize him.

The National Council of Churches of Christ adopted this resolution in 1964:

> The General Board of the National Council of Churches of Christ in the U.S.A., recognizing the ever-present danger of anti-Semitism, renews the call to the churches and the community to recognize (in the words of the First Assembly of the World Council of Churches) "anti-Semitism, no matter what its origin, is absolutely irreconcilable with the profession and practice of the Christian faith." The spiritual heritage of Jews and Christians should draw us to each other in obedience to the one Father and in continuing dialogue; the historic schism in our relations carries with it the need

for constant vigilance lest dialogue deteriorate into conflict. We confess that sometimes as Christians we have given way to anti-Semitism. We have even used the events of the Crucifixion to condemn the Jewish people whereas (in the words of the Third Assembly of the World Council of Churches) "the historic events which led to the Crucifixion should not be so presented as to fasten upon the Jewish people of today responsibilities which belong to our corporate humanity and not to one race or community."

The General Board urges that the members of the constituent communions seek that true dialogue with the religious bodies of the Jewish community through which differences of faith can be explored within the mutual life of the one family of God—separated, but seeking from God the gift of renewed unity—knowing that in the meantime God can help us to find our God-given unity in the common service of human need.

There have been additional statements from individual Protestant churches, such as the Lutheran World Federation and the House of Bishops of the Protestant Episcopal Church, both in 1964.

The Declaration on the Jews by the Second Vatican Council was approved on October 28, 1965. It arose from an earlier "schema" of 1962; at that earlier date the anticipated Declaration was to be alone; subsequently it became the fourth chapter of a broader decree, "The attitude of Catholics to non-Christians, especially the Jews." In the transition from the earlier schema to the adopted decree, the wording was altered, leading to the judgment of some Jews and Christians that the Declaration was weakened, but defended by others as not. There are minor differences in the English translations which have been published; the version here is from Cardinal Bea, *The Church and the Jewish People.*[1]

4. *Judaism*

As the Council searches into the mystery of the Church, it remembers the bond which spiritually ties the people of the New Covenant to the offspring of Abraham.

Thus the Church acknowledges that the beginnings of her faith and her election, according to God's saving design, are found already in the Patriarchs, Moses and the prophets. She professes that all who believe in Christ—Abraham's sons according to the faith (Cf. Galatians 3:7)—are included in the same Patriarch's call, and likewise that the salvation of the Church is symbolically prefigured in the exodus of the chosen people from the land of bondage. The Church, therefore, cannot forget that she received the revelation of the Old Testament through the people with whom God in his inexpressible mercy made the Ancient Covenant. Nor can she forget that she draws sustenance from the root of that well-cultivated olive tree onto which have been grafted the wild shoots, the Gentiles (Cf. Romans 11:17-24). Indeed, the Church believes that by his cross Christ our Peace reconciled Jews and Gentiles, making both one in himself (Cf. Ephesians 2:14-16).

The Church keeps ever in mind the words of the Apostle about his kinsman: "theirs is the sonship and the glory and the covenant and the law and the worship and the promises; theirs are the fathers and from them is the Christ according to the flesh" (Romans 9:4-5), the Son of the Virgin Mary.

[1] New York, 1966; pp. 150-153.

She also recalls that the Apostles, the Church's mainstay and pillars, as well as most of the early disciples who proclaimed the Gospel of Christ to the world, sprang from the Jewish people.

As Holy Scripture testifies, Jerusalem did not recognise the time of her visitation (Cf. Luke 19:44), nor did the Jews, in large number, accept the Gospel; indeed not a few opposed its spreading (Cf. Romans 11:28). Nevertheless, God holds the Jews most dear for the sake of their Fathers; he does not repent of the gifts he makes or of the calls he issues—such is the witness of the Apostle (Cf. Romans 11:28-29; cf. Dogmatic Constitution on the Church, *Lumen Gentium,* A.A.S., 57, 1965, p. 20). In company with the prophets and the same Apostle, the Church awaits that day, known to God alone, on which all peoples will address the Lord with a single voice and "serve him with one accord" (Zephaniah 3:9) (Cf. Isaiah 66:23; Psalm 65 (66): 4; Romans 11:11-32).

Since then the spiritual patrimony common to Christians and Jews is so great, the Council wishes to foster and commend mutual understanding and esteem. This will be the fruit above all, of biblical and theological studies and of brotherly dialogues.

True, the Jewish authorities and those who followed their lead pressed for the death of Christ (Cf. John 19:6); still, what happened in his passion cannot be charged against all the Jews, without distinction, then alive, nor against the Jews of today. Although the Church is the new People of God, the Jews should not be represented as rejected by God or accursed, as if this followed from the holy Scriptures. All should see to it, then, that in catechetical work and in the preaching of the word of God they teach nothing save what conforms to the truth of the Gospel and the Spirit of Christ.

Furthermore, in her rejection of every persecution against any man, the Church, mindful of the patrimony she shares with the Jews and led not by political reasons but by the Gospel's spiritual love, decries hatred, persecutions, manifestations of anti-Semitism, directed against Jews at any time and by anyone.

Besides, Christ out of infinite love freely underwent his passion and death for the sins of all men in order that all may reach salvation. This the Church has always taught and teaches still; and it is therefore the duty of the Church to proclaim the cross of Christ as the sign of God's all-embracing love and as the fountain from which every grace flows.

There are some characteristics in common in these statements. We Jews have welcomed them, even though the Declaration by the Second Vatican Council, through alterations in the language in the progress of the schema, has undergone considerable discussion, and evokes some criticism from both Jews and Christians. What is common in these statements is the repudiation of historic anti-Semitism and present-day anti-Semitism. Also, there is present in the Amsterdam Declaration and the Second Vatican Declaration the suggestion that Christians continue in the hope and intention of converting Jews to Christianity. It must be stated that some of us Jews have, indeed, raised the question as to whether these statements are designed to repudiate anti-Semitism in its own terms, or only to remove it as the barrier to success in converting us.

My own judgment runs along the following lines, that these statements are internal to Christendom, and the question of the wording and intention an intra-Christian matter. To the extent that these documents come into the arena of public attention, people are entitled to express judgments on them. But the issue, however much it may impinge on us Jews, is the business of you Christians, and of your Christian conscience.

Proselyting

The matter of your long-standing wish to convert us is as sensitive an issue as is the theme, so often imbedded in your literature, of the collective blame on all of us Jews for the crucifixion. If I understand right, you, from your standpoint, inherit as a basic motif in Christendom the mandate to be a missionary religion. The closing words of the Gospel according to Matthew are these: "Travel and teach all the nations, baptizing them in the name of the Father, and the Son, and the Holy Spirit, teaching them to observe all that I have commanded you." You call this passage the "Great Commission." You inherited this missionary impulse from Judaism; you carried it out with infinitely greater success. It is a dominant theme in your tradition, but is only a recessive one in ours; indeed, some of us Jews are quite unaware that our tradition includes a missionary impulse which predates yours, and that we Jews long ago had a somewhat extensive missionary movement, which fell into disuse.

We Jews have a special and central focus in your missionary efforts, for various New Testament passages seem to make us your highest priority. You often trace this mandate to Paul's Epistle to the Romans, especially Chapter 10. You maintain a host of special commissions and agencies designed to convert us; we do not maintain any designed to convert you. In the past you often resorted to forcible conversion, or gave us the choice of conversion or exile; on occasions our people were compelled to assemble to listen to conversionist addresses (and a heavy penalty fell on the Jew who put into his ear some barrier to hearing). You have wanted us, almost desperately, to convert, and you have resented us for not acquiescing.

If you ask us why we have ordinarily resisted conversion, the answer might be given in three reasons. First, we have not come to believe as you believe; it is that simple. You had adduced what for you is convincing proof that we should, this in the form of citations from the literature which you hold sacred but we do not, and therefore we have not been persuaded. Moreover, we have been at last a little surprised at your willingness to receive from us converts whose sincerity you carefully abstained from inquiring into, and to accept conversions for the convenience of the converts. We have continued to hold that we who do not believe with you should not join with you. This disinclination on our part to believe, you have, historically, attributed to a blindness on our part, while we have attributed it to some measure of integrity and clear-sightedness. Second, enough of us Jews, who joined with you Christians, thereafter said things about us and did things to us so as to constitute a record of infamous achievement. To cite only a few, men such as Nicholas Donin (France, 12th century), Pablo Christiani (France, 13th century), Abner of Burgos (Spain, 14th century), and Johann Pfefferkorn (Germany, 16th century), told unconscionable lies about the faith they had left, spurring Christians to cruelties and persecutions; in those ages in which we Jews had reason to fear you Christians, the apostates from us to you were infinitely more fearful to us than you yourselves. Your animosity had at least a certain sincerity, and even honesty about it, but these apostates did you no credit. We retain still today an anxiety about what apostates tell you about us, because of experiences of the past. The third reason lies in the methods, tactics, and procedures of many of your missionaries to us. Perhaps I can make this point more telling by citing a situation that has nothing to do with us Jews. An Indian state, Madhya Pradesh, appointed a commission to inquire into the activities of Christian missionaries. I quote from its recommendations:

> . . . Any attempt by force or fraud, or threats of illicit means or grants of financial or other aid, or by fraudulent means or promises, or by moral or material assistance, or by taking advantage of any person's inexperience or confidence, or by exploiting any person's necessity, spiritual weakness or thoughtlessness, or, in general, any attempt or effort (whether successful or not), directly or indirectly to penetrate into the religious conscience of persons (whether

of age or underage) of another faith, for the purpose of consciously altering their religious conscience or faith, so as to agree with the ideas or convictions of the proselyting party shall be absolutely prohibited. . . . An amendment of the Constitution of India may be sought, firstly to clarify that the right of propagation has been given only to the citizens of India, and secondly, that it does not include conversions brought about by force, or fraud, or other illicit means.[2]

If you ask, have your missionaries to us employed means comparable to those here discountenanced, then the honest answer must be Yes. The responsible among you have disowned these methods; they have needed disowning because they existed.

The facts are that, on the one hand, we do not want you to try to convert us but, on the other hand, the missionary motif is central in your tradition. Both you and we must take note of the presence, even in the laudable documents in which you repudiate anti-Semitism, of your continued adherence to the missionary motif. Can you carry on your purpose in such a way that it neither does violence to our dignity nor implies that you have abandoned this motif which you hold central? The answer lies in your hands, not in ours.

A few of your leaders, such as Reinhold Niebuhr in *Pious and Secular America,* have taken the stand that you Christians should abstain from the effort to convert us:

[2] Cited from Wilfred Cantwell Smith, *The Faith of Other Men* (New York, 1963), pp. 117-118.

Our analysis assumes that these [missionary] activities are wrong not only because they are futile and have little fruit to boast for their exertions. They are wrong because the two faiths despite differences are sufficiently alike for the Jew to find God more easily in terms of his own religious heritage than by subjecting himself to the hazards of guilt feeling involved in conversion to a faith which, whatever its excellencies, must appear to him as a symbol of an oppressive majority culture. . . . Practically nothing can purify the symbol of Christ as the image of God in the imagination of the Jew from the taint with which ages of Christian oppression in the name of Christ have tainted it.[3]

Stephen Neill, in *Christian Faith and Other Faiths,*[4] after quoting the above excerpt from Niebuhr, registers a dissent. He denies, by implication, that the fruits of the missionary effort to convert Jews have been as scarce as Niebuhr supposes, stating that almost all of you know about the case of individual Jews who have been successfully converted. He proceeds to make the point that Niebuhr's line of thought logically "would rule out almost every Christian attempt anywhere to win any adherent of another religion to faith in Christ." Lastly, Neill avers that "if the Jew can as satisfactorily find his way to God through Judaism, and the Hindu through Hinduism . . . what have Christians to preach, and why should they preach? The Christian mission springs from the conviction that Christ is *the* word of God, and that to have encountered God revealed in the

[3] New York, 1958; p. 108.
[4] New York, 1961.

face of Jesus Christ is to have entered into an experience wholly different from anything else that life can offer."

I have no idea to what extent you Christians would hold with Neill (who chances to be English) or with Niebuhr (who chances to be American). I would imagine that most of you American Christians would incline to Niebuhr, on the American premise that all religions are pretty good (or pretty bad), and the right to select whichever one a person wants is his individual and private concern.

When Neill speaks of Christianity as *the* word of God, he is asserting that Christianity is a better religion than any or all other religions.[5] Some of us Jews hold a comparable opinion about Judaism, as do Moslems about Islam. My own view is that any such opinion is an unseemly parochialism, and this is so whether it is held by a Jew, or a Christian, or a Moslem. What seems to elude Neill is that the inherent high quality, rather than some supposed superiority, can well serve to justify the maintenance of a particular tradition. In the same breath in which I would deny that Judaism is superior to Christianity, I would also deny that Christianity is superior to Judaism. Traditions can be described only as different, not as better or less good.

Both of our traditions contain the unhappy motif of

[5] Neill concedes that Christians may possibly have to alter the manner of the Christian approach, especially to eliminate the "suggestion that the Christians are givers and the Jews destined receivers. In our day we have to move forward a step further; we can think and speak only in terms of the dialogue between Jewry and the Church, between the old Israel and the New" (*op. cit.*, pp. 26-29).

superiority. Both, possessed of what we might term values, that is, admirable aspects, tend to confuse these values with objective truth, and to regard the facets of one's own tradition as necessarily interchangeable with demonstrated validity and absolute truth. Many of us Jews are alert to the irrational in your tradition and blind to it in our own; many of you Christians are alert to the glories in your tradition, and prone to scorn our ways. This latter is a serious charge, and I must therefore document it.

Your conviction of your superiority to us begins in the New Testament which you, of course, deem sacred and authoritative, but which all too often you tend to forget we do not. A usual New Testament view runs along the following line, that there is a long history of the various times in the remote past when God disclosed himself, as to the patriarchs and the prophets; the climax of that history of divine disclosure took place in God's revelation in Christ. This latter revelation is, from your standpoint, not only more recent, but more climactic, and hence superior and supreme.

Moreover—and here for clarity I repeat material I have touched on above—the nub of Judaism consisted centrally of laws, the Mosaic laws, which are to be found beginning in Exodus 20. The patriarchs, however, lived before the age of Moses, and were presumably not subject to the Mosaic laws, but they managed nevertheless to attain religious rightness; such was the case with Abraham who "believed in the Lord and He reckoned it unto him as righteousness." Paul believed that with the advent of the Christ, man was enabled again to achieve righteousness in the way that the patriarchs had, without recourse to laws; Christians have invariably held that for attaining righteousness, "faith" is a superior vehicle to laws (even though, inconsistently, Christians have developed their own canon or denominational laws).

It is very hard for us Jews to understand Paul (let alone to agree with him!), for there is in our tradition nothing that resembles Paul's derogation and abrogation of the laws.[6] Indeed, I wish I could suggest inoffensively just how alien and irreverent the views of Paul appear to most Jews, especially since we do not hold Paul's teachings to be sacred.[7]

Invidious Comparisons

An easy contrast has existed in which more of your thinkers and writers have applauded "faith" and scorned "laws"; and these thinkers and writers extol Christianity as a very pure religion which chanced to

[6] In my *The Genius of Paul,* I noted a tendency somewhat similar, though nevertheless different, in the pre-exilic prophets.

[7] I find it difficult at times to persuade fellow Jews that Paul is not the only voice in the New Testament. Indeed, in my book on Paul, which assesses him as a great religious genius, I struggled to make him clear to Jewish readers; from this standpoint the book represents a significant failure, for most Jews who read it seem to find my "clear" exposition quite as unintelligible as Paul's Epistles themselves; one recalls the passage, II Peter 3:16, which speaks of Paul's Epistles as "hard to understand."

emerge from that tangled web of pathetic legalism called Judaism. I do not here exaggerate, and I do not here have in mind the medieval Christian foes who were ignoramuses, and who spoke of Judaism not as a religion but elegantly as a superstition and inelegantly as vomit. I speak here of supposedly responsible Christian scholars in our own century. I will ask you to accept two quotations as typical, and request that you take my assurance that I could supply an endless series of examples. William Fairweather, in *The Background of the Gospels,*[8] writes:

> The Spirit of the later Judaism is different from that of the prophets. . . . The prophets preached the necessity of justice, mercy, and humility . . . the [rabbinic] teachers of the people insisted upon the most punctilious discharge of every ceremonial ordinance, even where that might mean neglect of moral duties. . . . There was no sense of spiritual proportion tending to frame life into a moral unity. . . . A further feature of Jewish ethic as conditioned by the Law is its narrow particularism. . . . In Judaism, therefore, we have an unsuccessful attempt to establish religion on an ethical basis. It needed only the magnetic touch of Jesus to call into operation what was already dormant in the community. . . . The lack of creative originality . . . characterized [this] period, and also the lack of great religious personalities like Moses or Samuel, Origen or Augustine, Luther or Knox, around whom the life and history of their own generation revolves. . . .

The second example occurs in an essay, "Judaism, the

[8] Edinburgh, 1920, 3rd edition, p. 157.

Religion in which Christ was Educated," by the Rev. Canon David Capell Simpson:[9]

> Christian theologians . . . though too often ignorant of Hebrew and Aramaic, and therefore without first-hand knowledge of the pertinent literature in its true setting, have at times rashly supposed themselves competent to dogmatize alike on primitive Christianity and on its Jewish background.

There ensues Simpson's description of the various facets of Judaism prior to the time of Jesus. Yet here is how Simpson concludes his essay (p. 171):

> But for His [Christ's] revelation, Judaism would have continued as the noblest attempt made by man to apprehend the Divine and to translate high ideals into actions. As it was, Judaism played an essential part not only in educating humanity to receive His revelation, but also in His own education. . . . But, having done so, it was . . . unable to see the true magnitude of its work. . . . Like many a human parent it failed to grasp that its child was at least full grown, and that *its own task was then completed* [the italics are mine].

I think you can understand that we Jews do not respond favorably to the suggestion that our religion is outmoded and passé, and secondary in quality to yours, or that it became negligible in significance when once your religion arose.

We can go on and read those textbooks that tell us that we Jews conceive of God as a harsh ruler, but you

[9] *The History of Christianity in the Light of Modern Knowledge: a Collective Work* (London and Glasgow, 1929), chapter VI.

Christians conceive of Him as a loving father. Ours is a God of vengeance, yours of forgiveness—though it is the same God! You espouse love, a worthy quality, and we justice, a lesser quality. And so on. But there is no point in multiplying such examples, which are abundant. Let me say, with considerable reserve, that this sort of thing represents bias and incorrect scholarship. The proof of this latter statement rests on the turn of the tide in Christian scholarship itself since the work of an American Presbyterian, George Foot Moore[10] (1851-1931). He has been followed by a succession of eminent Protestant scholars who with honesty and with admirable courage have corrected and reformed the tradition of writing about Judaism of which Fairweather is typical. You will not read a shabby treatment of Judaism in your best Christian scholars any more, but you can still read it among those who are not your best. And, unhappily, you can still read the unreliable with great frequency in popular studies.

But, rather than refute the distortions of Judaism, let me substitute for a more affirmative description of Judaism what lawyers call a demurrer. Accordingly, let me concede for the moment that these adverse appraisals are true and not the distortions they are. We Jews

[10] Two significant works relate to this. His three-volume *Judaism in the First Centuries of the Christian Era* (Cambridge, 1927-1930), was preceded by his "Christian Writers on Judaism," *Harvard Theological Review*, Vol. 14 (1921), pp. 197-254. In this latter he reviewed and sharply criticized what he regarded as ignorant or partisan denigrations of Judaism; his book is an example of scholarship at its best, in terms of its reliability, its objectivity, its accuracy, and its clarity.

by now know a little of your Christian history, and some of us can admire your great achievements. But do you ever read what Luther wrote about the Catholic Church, and what Catholics before Pope John XXIII wrote about Luther? Shall we Jews admire the manner in which Henry VIII detached the Church of England from the Church at Rome? May an outsider to Christianity mention tactfully such things as the Thirty Years' War, St. Bartholomew's Night, and the executions of John Hus, of Giordano Bruno, and of Michael Servetus, performed by Christians against Christians, in the name of Christianity? May I mention the now defunct Index of Prohibited Books? Would you understand that some of us Jews, even accepting Fairweather's judgment, would be willing to let his disparaging appraisal of us be weighed in the balance against portions of the Christian record? In this light, can you reasonably expect us to acquiesce in the judgment that your religion is superior to ours? Has it bred better people? Has it determined the issues of peace and war, and prosperity and tranquillity among Christian nations? (I find moments in which my Jewish loyalty finds comfort in the circumstance that we never had the privilege in western Europe of Judaism's being as flaunted by our people as your tradition has been by yours; had we had the chance, my reading of the Maccabean age, especially about the latter kings, persuades me that our record would have been no better than yours has been.)

But no, your religion, great and admirable as it is, is

different from ours, not better. Ours is different from yours, not better.

But I imagine that while some of you and some of us will get to the point of describing our religions merely as different, and immune from judgment as to superior and inferior, we who do so will remain a minority in both traditions.[11] Religion unhappily seems to evoke this untenable and distasteful chauvinism. It is certain, however, that assertions of superiority in the one will prompt counterassertions of superiority in the other, and that in the array of assertions and counterassertions, each religion will undergo distortion and disparagement at the hands of the other. And men who feel no loyalty for or interest in either tradition will be treated to the spectacle of religions maligning each other, this in the name of religion.

It is obviously true that within each of our traditions there are the sacred literatures which provide, at least on the surface, a sanction for the one or the other to feel superior to the other, or to everybody else. Such literature, possessing more that is affirmative than negative, has weight and authority, and hence for us today to adopt an attitude at variance with these sentiments

[11] Wilfred Cantwell Smith, *The Faith of Other Men* (New York, 1963; p. 90), writes, respecting Jews and Christians, on the one hand, and other traditions: "The dominant tradition in Christian theology has tended to take the line that other men's faith is, without discussion, false; that in other religious traditions outside the Christian, or outside the Jewish and Christian, you have men seeking God, which they are incapable of doing successfully, while only in our own do you have God seeking men, revealing and giving Himself—so that religious truth and true faith are exclusively here."

which arose in ancient times presents something of a problem. Thus, for us Jews there is the problem that our Scripture and the subsequent rabbinic literature speak of us as a chosen people. If we are indeed chosen, then one might infer that everybody else is not chosen. Manifestly, the ancient texts cannot be changed. Manifestly, religious communities are not going to cast away their sacred texts. A way out of the dilemma is customarily found in the area of *interpretation,* that is, in the way in which men of a later age can extract some worthy and favorable meaning out of passages which on the surface have an opposite import. For example, those of us Jews who reject theories of "racial" superiority, reject them relating to ourselves too; a customary procedure among us is to say, about being chosen, that it was a choice made for obligation, that we were chosen to serve, not for privilege; or, as some among us have said, we chose God rather than He chose us. That is to say, the procedure is not to change ancient Scriptures, but to make them take on affirmative meanings.

In the New Testament there are passages which are hostile to Jews and Judaism. There is this discernible difference among you, that a good many of you Protestants acknowledge the presence of these passages, explain them as products of the age of antagonism in which they were written and repudiate for all time the anti-Jewish sentiment in them. The Catholics among you seem averse to imputing ignoble sentiments to the New Testament, and the Catholic procedure is to assert that these passages have been misunderstood or misinterpreted in the past, and require proper understanding today, and then go on to explain the import of these passages in such a way that they lose the weight of the anti-Jewish flavor. In this difference between you Protestants and you Catholics, Protestants are willing to admit that there is anti-Jewish substance in the New Testament, and Catholics not. Moreover, Protestants have been willing to challenge the historical accuracy (not alone the supposed *theological* validity) of the New Testament (and the Old), but Catholics unwilling. You Christians are thus separated from each other concerning the full facts, or the exact facts, about the crucifixion, and about how much responsibility the Jews of the age of Jesus had in the execution of Jesus. Your scholars usually agree that it was the Romans who did the crucifying. The disagreement is on the extent of Jewish responsibility at that time for the Roman deed. Protestant scholars usually discern in the successive documents a shift of blame from the Romans to the Jews, with the upshot that the Christian documents reflect for them an entire exoneration of the Romans, and in artificial incrimination of the Jews, even beyond the tiny portion of the Jews participating, and extending instead to all the Jews; such Protestant scholars tend to regard the motif in the Christian Scriptures of Jewish responsibility for the crucifixion as theological, and not historical. That is to say, a good many of your Protestant scholars are willing to deny the validity of the historical statements in the Gospels, while your Catholic scholars are not; your Catholic scholars tend rather to *interpret* the material so as to free it from religious animosity, but to retain the historical validity of the Gospel passages. I think that you will find it easy to see why we Jews have a preference for the procedure of the Protestant scholars, even while we welcome the tone of the Catholic interpretations. Some of us Jews, perhaps a little insensitive about the bonds which tie you to your Christian Scriptures, intimate or even suggest that you ought to alter your Scriptures, and, naturally, you regard this sort of thing as no less than blasphemy. Perhaps most of you are unaware of the occasional statement by a Jew that so long as there is a New Testament, there will always be anti-Jewish sentiment in segments of Christendom. (Such Jews often seem to know the New Testament only to the extent of this one theme.) The usual reply from among you is that, first, you have no intention of casting aside or altering the New Testament, and second, that it is only the misunderstanding of it that can find a sanction for anti-Jewish feeling in it. Some of you add, as you can and should, that there are passages in the New Testament which enjoin the unreserved love by man of his fellow man.

There are, of course, those among you who continue to find a sanction in the New Testament for anti-Jewish feeling, and who believe that they are obligated to be in accord with that Scriptural sanction.

I know of no real way of resolving this matter of the content of sacred writings to the fullest satisfaction of all concerned. Many of your churches, here and abroad, have been scrupulously careful that your new religious school textbooks omit the disparagement of Jews and Judaism which marked your older textbooks; in this matter, many of you have been most zealous. I believe that many, perhaps most of you, can and will rid yourselves of animosity to us. I also believe that you are finding that this matter of a scriptural sanction for scorning or despising us is one of your abiding problems.

As to the question of religions being superior or only different, this is my opinion as I find it in history: Judaism underwent inner development after Christianity was born and therefore I believe that historic Christianity and Judaism reflect parallel developments from the Judaism which existed at the time of the birth of Christianity. You Christians, on the one hand, identifying Jesus as the Messiah, and concluding that the laws of Moses were abrogated, based your religion on faith, on belief in the saving acts of the Christ; we Jews, on the other hand, have continued to regard the laws of Moses as binding, and have developed and amplified these laws, and we believe the Messiah has not yet come. Involved here is deep difference, not objective superiority or inferiority.

From Pagan to Christian Anti-Semitism

Anti-Jewish feeling is older than Christianity. From the circumstance that it existed in the Greco-Roman world prior to the time of the birth of Christianity, some of you are prone to regard anti-Jewish feeling as independent of the Christian sentiment, and attribute it to our exclusiveness, or to other character defects, and thereby you tend to exempt Christianity from any burden of responsibility. Anti-Jewish feeling, however, though admittedly pre-Christian, rested on considerations more complex than mere exclusiveness. That exclusiveness itself was the result of the peculiar political and social anomalies in the Greco-Roman world, whereby Jews were permitted to retain Jewish laws and practices within the Dispersion areas, *as were other migrant peoples*. It rested on Jewish religious separatism, for Jews declined to adopt or succumb to paganism. That is, Jews paid a price for their religious loyalty.

What many of you seem to need to learn from your scholars is that you have a rich heritage of a Christian martyrology simply because you Christians took exactly the same attitude to paganism that we Jews did, and you evoked the same antagonism along with us, for pagans often could not tell the difference between you and us. You too kept yourselves apart from paganism. We Jews find it a little hard to understand why religious loyalty is obnoxious when it is ours, and laudable when it is yours.

When you became the official religion in the Roman empire, you extirpated all the other religions so that none of the pagan religions survived. (You inherited this intolerance from us, and you extended it.) By absorbing the pagans into your corporate body, you ceased to need separation from them. But you must not now misread the records, as if the pagans hated us but not you. Do you not see that in your absorbing the pagans within you, you added your religious sanction to the already existing sociological antagonisms on the part of pagans that previously had been directed against both of us?

I note from time to time that you incline to a method of explaining things which is hard for me to grasp, even though I think I can paraphrase it correctly. A view is frequent among you in which you conceive of "the church" [12] as a kind of supernatural or ideal entity, one which is necessarily free from all defect. While the totality of you Christians constitute "the church," there is a sense in which "the church" is something other than and above the mere sum total of you who are Christians. You carry this distinction at times to one of contrast, that is, between the "invisible" church and the "visible." When there has emerged in history something kindred to a blemish, you take the line that it is a blemish in churchmen, but not in "the church." I heard it once put in this way, that it was churchmen who condemned Giordano Bruno to death, but not "the church." Similarly, I have heard it set forth that churchmen have been guilty of anti-Jewish actions, but never "the church." Can you understand that, with respect to past history, I find this distinction difficult to grasp, and even more difficult to assent to? Perhaps my difficulty

[12] In the phrase "Catholic Church," the first letter of each word would be capitalized as a proper noun; church, beginning with a small "c," refers to Christendom in general, and not to a specific communion.

is that we Jews lack a distinction of this kind, for we lack a comparable concept of "the synagogue." I think that the particular difficulty for me here is that I can see a sense in which you want to express the idea that your communicants, including your highest officials, can fall short of your religious ideals (as can ours); but when I read in a single sentence the assertion that anti-Semitism is pre-Christian, and also that "the church" is free of this taint, then I wonder if this combination is some device for diminishing the responsibility for the past record of persecution which has prompted your recent Declarations. On two occasions I have heard priests say something to this effect, that though Christians have persecuted, "the church" has not. Perhaps this is an effort to express the thought that Christians have fallen humanly short of the standards of Christianity (just as Jews fall short of Jewish ideals).

Perhaps the inference is to be drawn that neither persecution nor theological disparagement represents "the church"; but I am left to wonder if "the church," being thus unmarked by the history of its communicants, is prepared to address us Jews as if it regards our Judaism or anyone as equally worthy with itself. If "the church," and it alone, represents the ideal, then everything else is less than the ideal and "dialogue" becomes less than complete.

Limits to Religious Understanding

Somehow, I become less and less sure that full *religious* understanding is a realizable goal, especially on any broad basis between your men in the pews and ours. I do not mean that animosities cannot be largely reduced, and often eliminated, and that cooperation in common social ventures cannot increase. But the more I try to press on to envisage genuine and profound religious *understanding,* involving facts, ideas, and a fair and balanced comprehension of them, the more I become persuaded that parochialism and particularism can never completely disappear, for they strike me as so deeply imbedded as to defy eradication. I must risk offending by saying that you Christians tend to regard your Christianity as a pure universalism, but I wonder if your judgment here is sound and fair. In our Jewish tradition we have had eras of universalism and of particularism; with us the universalism has never extended to the point of liquidating the particular, nor the particularism ever to completely obliterating the universalism. I suspect that you are not any more universalistic than we are, but have merely substituted a new entity, "the church," or "Christendom," or "Christianity" for our inherited entity, the Jewish people. However universalistically you may reinterpret the phrase, "there is no salvation except in the church," the phrase remains, and I imagine that you will concede that there are those among you who hold to the literal import of the phrase, however much you differ on which denomination is to be regarded as "the church." I am by no means sure how far to universalism all of us Jews will go, for though I know that some will go a long way, I know that others will go scarcely any distance.

There is, of course, the possibility that within the confines of inevitable particularism, some individual persons can nevertheless be universalistic. If so, they are this way not because of the tradition, Jewish or Christian, but despite it. Indeed, when such universalistic persons arise, their impulses are apt to be humanistic, that is to say, the product of heightened humane qualities rather than the result of a religious mandate. Men are mixtures in many ways, and it seems to me possible therefore that a man can be fully universalistic, even while adhering to a tradition which by its nature falls short of perfect universalism.

Our Common World

You and we share together in modern culture. There is a minor problem that arises for us, the issue of a distinction between Christian and secular as it relates to this culture. It is not too difficult to define either term at the point of its extreme. Thus, when one has in mind Christian beliefs, worship services, and ritual, that is all clear enough. When one has in mind the facets of modern culture which are totally disconnected from Christianity, such as mathematics or polytonal music or space exploration, this too is clear enough. But there is a large area between, in which the general humanism of the past centuries lies and where the distinction is not so clear. On the one hand, the liturgical music of Bach, Mozart, and Beethoven is both Christian and also in a sense a portion of Western man's cultural heritage;

on the other hand, certain emphases on personal freedom which have taken on secular form are derived from specifically Christian convictions (although some Christians have set themselves as obstacles to such freedom even for other Christians, as, for example, the limitation on Protestants in some Catholic land). Though our modern civilization is a secular one, it is marked by a strong coloration of elements that are derived directly from Christendom and, one step back, from Judaism; that is why the phrase "Judeo-Christian" has arisen to describe the spiritual note often present in the ethical criteria normally endorsed by modern man.

Jews are no longer strangers to this modern culture, as they were in ghetto days. Almost unanimously they regard it as a portion of their own spiritual patrimony. It comes about, accordingly, that Jews, abstaining from accepting an influence that comes directly from Christianity, accept it when it is mediated by modern humanistic culture. Hence, both Jews and Christians live in a world which is non-Christian and at the same time permeated by facets of Christianity. So intermixed are these elements that they often defy isolation from each other. On the most superficial level, Sunday is a day of rest for Jews as it is for Christians, and secular as the day has become, and abundantly as Christians may absent themselves from church services, the day is almost universally a day of rest. A handful of Jews in Western countries make the attempt to shield themselves not only from Christianity but also from that entity I have called modern culture; similarly, there are

Christians who in a different but quite similar way shield themselves. But most of us, you Christians and we Jews, live in a world in which we each carry the dual citizenship of our religion and of modern culture. There is no such thing as Jewish mathematics or Christian chemistry. We Jews read the same novels, watch the same television programs, attend the same concerts, and vote in the same elections as you Christians. We are bearers of the same modern culture, but we bear it in accordance with individual tastes and prepossessions, not as Jews or as Christians.

We inhabit the same secular world, and yet for some portion of time we each cultivate something which is apart, separate from this same world. How shall we regard these separations? Are they analogous and parallel to each other? We in our way and you in yours have religious standards which we both invoke to shield us from the vice in the world, and which prompt us to express judgments on these vices. Even when we recognize the presence of an ethical element within secular society, along with its vice, we each feel the need of a special, religious consecration to ethics, and consequently of religious communities of people who can be undeviatingly loyal to our common ethics. Neither you nor we can be estranged from the world, and yet if we are to be of benefit to mankind, we need deliberately to cultivate that legacy in our religions which, if it disappeared, would be a loss to mankind. We are not the sole benefactors of mankind, for nonreligious humanists are also to be regarded as benefactors. Potentially our religions still have much to offer, both to our own communicants and also to mankind. It would be tragic for the world if either or both of us were dissolved and disappeared. I contend this even though I am aware of that part of the past record that must be described as blemished.

If there is reason for both our religions, even with their blemishes, to be perpetuated, then how shall they regard each other? How can we respect each other, cooperate with each other, understand each other?

In all candor, the road to religious understanding involves more than the admirable ability merely to rise above parochialism. If the word "understanding" is to be taken with any seriousness, then there is necessarily involved a need for disciplined academic study. This implies spending thoughtful attention on writings about history, about theology, about sociology. There does not exist any corps of scholars who have as yet gone beyond elementary pioneering stages in the study by us of you or of you by us. A mere handful of us Jews have studied the New Testament in any seriousness, and even fewer have delved into the subsequent periods of Christian history. While I know of a few Christians who have studied the ancient rabbinic Judaism, I know of only two who ever studied it for its own sake and in its own terms. Some scholars have studied particular, limited areas or topics, such as medieval relations, or the sociology of urban Jewish communities. Yet it is necessary to report that we have so far made only a beginning in the academic study of Jewish-Christian relationships.

Such study, ideally, would be objective, profound, and thorough. It is urgently needed, and it has a very, very great distance still to go.

Academic study inevitably involves technicalities which are not readily susceptible of conveyance to the general public. Only a portion, only a limited distillation of its main themes can be responsibly conveyed. The proper and full understanding is therefore apt to be the possession of the specialists. What they learn and teach can in time be conveyed from scholar to clergyman, and then distilled to the pew. This sort of development could reasonably be expected.

Yet we must sadly admit that there are many people who have little or no thirst to learn, and are bereft of any desire to unlearn and relearn. Some of you and some of us will remain content to be free of any interest in understanding each other, preferring each his own particularism. A larger group, among both you and us, seems to me animated by the desire to appreciate, but has neither the will nor the tools for an accompanying comprehension. I personally find no despair in the latter, for to my mind the prologue to the academic, technical study of our religion by you, or yours by us, requires first of all a climate favorable to such study; this climate has begun to exist because your laymen and ours predominantly want it to exist. Accordingly, though many of you and many of us possibly may never reach full religious understanding of each other, if we can only grasp that you and we, as human beings, are creatures not only of the same flesh and blood but of the same spiritual idealism and dedication, albeit differently directed, that might well be recognition enough. If we constantly remind ourselves that we are too much accustomed to conceive of unknown men in terms of stereotypes, and too much inclined to overlook the unique individuality that each of us possesses, we could increase in wisdom. I know many Christians, and no two of them are identical; I know many more Jews, and no two of them are identical. A heightened human warmth, and sympathy, and the willingness to inquire about each other could be gain enough.

7

JEWISH ATTITUDE: GUIDANCE FROM OUR PAST

A backward glance through these chapters would yield this picture of us Jews and our community as you Christians see it today: In the shift from the medieval scene to the recent and then the present, many of the social and economic separatisms constraining Jews have disappeared. We Jews now have the rights of full citizenship in most, though not all, Western countries. Most of us Jews, though not quite all of us, are fully attuned to the Western secular culture, with its science, its literature, its social movements; a very good many of us as individuals (that is, not specifically as Jews) have made outstanding contributions to the totality of modern civilization. At one time Christianity persecuted us; religious persecution largely has disappeared, and the tragedy of the Hitler period was essentially "pseudo-racism," rather than religious.

We have a religious tradition to which most of us remain undeviatingly loyal, but that loyalty exists today in a variety of forms and of intensities, ranging from fullest synagogal affiliation and participation, through the merely formal, to the absence of any fervent affiliation. And we live in the midst of transitions which are incomplete and of changes which began relatively recently. We Jews are an entity of some kind, though it is somewhat difficult to find the exact term to describe it, for, in Western countries, we are something kindred to a loose community of religious communicants, and yet some of us have fashioned and maintained a political entity, the State of Israel.[1] As a more or less corporate body, we Jews have our organizations, some of them similar to Christian corporate bodies, though some of them not. We have first of all local synagogues; we maintain various kinds of systems of religious education. We support hospitals and old folks' homes. We maintain establishments which we call Y.M.H.A.'s or

[1] To be completely clear, let me state that I am not an Israeli, I am an American. I have a deep concern for my fellow Jews who are Israelis, and from that standpoint a concern for their government, of which I am no part and which in no way claims the allegiance I owe and give to Washington. I served in the American Navy, not the Israeli, and I vote in Cincinnati, not in Tel Aviv. There is a range of matters, religious, social, literary, musical, scholarly, which Israelis cultivate. To some of this range, such as the scholarship, I feel close; to other portions I feel no closeness at all, even to the point of disinterest. What goes on in Israel represents a small portion of my total interests, with the largest portions focusing on the United States. I am deeply involved in matters of Judaism, but as a professional student rather than as one active in organizations. I am just as deeply involved in the welfare of the general American academic world as in the Jewish world.

Jewish Centers. We have fraternal orders, social clubs, and cultural associations. We maintain philanthropies, domestic and also those dedicated to the welfare of co-religionists in other countries. Most of us who do not reside in Israel are at the same time undeviatingly loyal nationals of the countries of our residence, and also deeply concerned for the welfare of individual Jews in Israel and for the State of Israel. In a country such as the United States, we have no legally recognized collective status, and wish none, but are instead individuals who exercise the right to unite our efforts for the good of our own people; again as individuals we participate in the common efforts for the good of all people.

The Detached View

Let us grant that in the premodern periods of religious persecution, when we were not free to take part in efforts for the good of all people, we Jews responded in a quite expected way of bitterness toward Christians. We need now to inquire whether or not there was, and is, some recurring theme among our best Jewish minds which reflects a thoughtful appraisal of Christianity, a theme which can be said to arise in some detachment from the press of immediate circumstance, rather than from intuitive response. There was and is such a recurring theme; I therefore proceed to cite how it appears among some of our eminent sages.

I turn first to Judah Ha-Levi (about 1075-1141) who lived in Spain in both Moslem and Christian towns (the Catholic reconquest of Spain was still only in process). He was a physician, a poet, and a philosopher. His philosophical book is called *The Kusari*, that is, "The Khazar." It supposes that a king of the Asiatic Khazars has invited before him four scholars, a Jew, a Christian, a Moslem, and an Aristotelian, to engage in a disputation on the question of the true religion, so that the king may know which of the four views to accept.[2] *The Kusari* necessarily dealt with the question of how Judaism regarded Christianity and Islam. The gist of Ha-Levi's view is that the younger religions accepted the roots of the Jewish faith, though not the logical inferences from them. On the one hand, as he comments, the younger religions amalgamated pagan rites and ideas into their respective traditions, and therefore Jews cannot go along with them; on the other hand, both Christianity and Islam form preparatory steps to the future Messianic era, and at that ultimate and ripened time the adherents of the younger religions will share in the Messianic benefits as branches of a single tree (prophesied about, according to Ha-Levi, in Ezekiel 37:17).[3]

Similarly, Moses Maimonides (1135-1204) was a physician, a legal scholar, a scientist, and a philosopher. He was born in Spain but settled in Egypt. Among his writings was the systematization of Jewish legalism in fourteen parts known as *Mishnah Torah* ("Recapitula-

[2] Ha-Levi has the king ultimately make the decision to accept Judaism; historically the kingdom of the Khazars, a tribe kindred to the Finns and the Turks, living in the region in Russia near the Volga delta, had converted to Judaism around the year 800.

[3] The principal references are *The Kusari,* I, 5 and IV, 11.

tion of the Revelation") and also as *Yad Hazaka* ("Strong Hand").[4] He goes somewhat beyond Ha-Levi in that he adds this note, that Christianity and Islam spread the words of Scripture and "the law of truth" over the whole earth. He comments that in the Messianic age, Christians and Moslems would turn to "the full truth." In another place (*Responsa* 58) he declares that, in common with the Jews, the Christians believe that the Bible is divine and was given through Moses; moreover, Christians possess it and in a written form.[5] He adds, in the interest of honesty, that Christians interpret the Bible differently from Jews.

Among a line of Jewish scholars[6] there appears a rather consistent and recurring view which repeats the essence of the statements of Ha-Levi and Maimonides. Joseph Caro seems to introduce a somewhat new note, and indeed, a new term; he states that Christians are not to be regarded as "idolators" (in spite of their worship of idols), but rather as "proselytes of the gate." Caro seems not informed about the great intra-Christian controversy in the 8th century over idols which added to the strains between the Eastern (Byzantine) church and the Western (Roman), for the East set about to abolish idol worship; this deep difference is

[4] The principal reference in *Yad Hazaka* is XI, 4; see also *Responsa* 58.

[5] That is to say, Mohammedans only hearken back to the Bible through allusions to it, but did not possess it.

[6] Gershom of Mayence (died 1040); Isaac of Troyes (known as Rashi) (1040-1105); Solomon ibn Adret of Barcelona (1235-1319); Isaac ben Sheshet Garfat (1328-1408); Joseph Caro (1488-1575); and Moses Isserles (1525-1572).

known in Christian history as the "iconoclast controversy," and had its distant echoes in various parts of the Christian world, especially after the Reformation period, when other Christians rejected idols. As to "proselytes of the gate,"[7] the phrase is medieval and has not been discovered in any document prior to the 13th century. The ancient rabbinic literature had distinguished between "proselytes" and "semi-proselytes" —the latter probably meaning pagan men sympathetic to Judaism but unprepared to undergo circumcision. It is likely that the medieval phrase "proselytes of the gate" was intended to distinguish between pagans and Christians. When Caro termed Christians to be "proselytes of the gates," his intention was to evaluate them as infinitely closer to Judaism than were pagans, and to regard them, accordingly, as quite distinct from pagans.

One additional passage is even more explicit than all the preceding. It comes from Jacob Emden (1697-1776) of northern Germany; it is, however, paralleled in sentiment by other rabbis of the general period. He writes: "Christianity has been given to the Gentile world by the Apostles as part of the Jewish religion; and its founder has even made the moral laws stricter than those contained in Mosaism.[8] There are, accordingly, many Christians of high qualities and excellent morals who abstain from hatred and do no harm, even to their enemies. Would that Christians would all live

[7] On the phrase, see George Foot Moore, *Judaism* I, 341 and III, 112.

[8] This is an allusion to Matthew 5:21-48, wherein, in seven matters, the attitude of Jesus is stricter than that of Moses.

in conformity with their precepts! They are not enjoined, like the Jews, to observe the laws of Moses; nor do they sin if they associate other beings with God in worshipping a triune God. They will receive reward from God for having propagated a belief in Him among nations that never heard His name. . . ."

These statements are each individual, and they are edifying, rather than obligatory or binding. To be sure, one can cull, especially from periods of persecutions, sentiments by Jews which are the reverse of these. Nevertheless, these attitudes constitute a kind of chain of calm and judicious appraisal by leading Jewish minds of Christianity and Christians.

None of these statements comes from the modern age. The one-volume *Standard Jewish Encyclopedia* (rev. ed., 1966) contains this statement (p. 441): "Some outstanding Christian teachers of the 19th and 20th centuries opposed anti-Semitism as essentially un-Christian. In the US and, to some extent, in W[estern] Europe there has been interfaith activity intended to bring about better understanding and joint activity by church and synagogue groups for civic betterment and social justice."

In the 19th and 20th centuries there were a number of Jews who expressed attitudes about Christianity in this same vein as the medieval luminaries. An outstanding example is Franz Rosenzweig (1886-1929), a German who, when a soldier in the German army during World War I, wrote *Stern der Erlösung* ("Star of Redemption"). A living Jewish scholar, Jacob Katz, has epitomized the view of Rosenzweig, and of other 19th-century Jews, as signifying this, that Christianity is to be viewed, affirmatively, as the religion for the Gentiles, all Gentiles, while Judaism is the religion for Jews. The supposition in this conclusion rests on the premise of the equal validity of the two religions, with the implication that the essential difference is in the people who carry the religions.

Amalgamation?

Sometimes the question is asked: Are there on record any proposals, direct and unmistakable ones, which would envisage, rather than "peaceful coexistence," actual conditions under which something no less than merger would take place? I know of no direct or unmistakable proposals, but there are on record some vague, indistinct, and indirect expressions in that general direction, coming primarily from Germany in the latter part of the 18th and the early part of the 19th centuries. For example, one Jew proposed that he and other Jews were prepared to "accept" Jesus, but only as a man, not as divine. Such proposals failed to be taken with any seriousness, for they represented pious generalities rather than specific programs, and they presupposed that each tradition would undergo notable alterations and reductions, thereby to furnish some least common denominator for the two. I would take it that we Jews do not now, any more than we did then, seriously envisage merger with Christendom, nor you

Christians with us. I suggest, rather, that the two religions can and must live amicably side by side, each possessing its array of values and of individual components, which express with some adequacy the values inherited from the past and which are agreeable to the disposition of the ongoing communicants. The absorbing of either faith by the other is an idea no more sensible than the merging. While a few among us Jews are persuaded of the superiority of Judaism to Christianity, this view does not mark most of us; we would be impelled to deny the superiority of Judaism over Christianity in the same breath that we would deny the superiority of Christianity over Judaism.

A combination of both partiality for one's own tradition along with a fair-minded assessment of the values of parallel traditions may be too new for many of you, as for many of us. It is, however, an inescapable necessity when we find ourselves in a shrunken world where there are religions which are neither Christianity nor Judaism, and which can no longer be ignored in the framework of collective mankind. More of us and more of you seem faced with the need to learn that fidelity to one's own tradition need not lead to arrogance about it, or to distorting the significance or the true content of religions not our own.

Deterrents to Assessment

We Jews in the modern world have tended toward a view of the relative equality of all religions.

Your religion was born within ours, and left it, and there exist some elements which you and we have in common and some which are quite diverse. A Jewish attitude toward Christianity, then, must simultaneously take cognizance of the relationship of parent to offspring and of the abiding integrity of both parent and offspring. *In this connection, we must momentarily forget the centuries of persecution and disabilities because they are not germane to the deep and abiding question of a Jewish attitude to Christianity. In any profound inquiry, the persecution and disabilities need to be regarded as kindred to the accident of history which obscure the true questions. Let us try to imagine that Christians had never scorned or persecuted us; in that light, what would our attitude be to a religion born among us, which left us?*

Respecting the persecutions, it is every bit as wrong for one of us to blame one of you today for what happened to our forebears in those dreadful incidents in Spain in 1492, in Poland in 1648, in Russia in 1903 and 1905, as for you to blame us for the crucifixion of Jesus. It is equally wrong to hold American Christians responsible for what ostensible Christians who were Nazis did to Jews in Europe during what we Jews call the "holocaust." All this needs to be unmistakably clear, and it needs to remain clear even though when one of us is rebuffed or reviled as a *Jew* by one of you, he may inevitably associate many or all of you with the past record of events.

In thinking of our relationships, we must avoid still

another unfortunate kind of attitude, the mention of which will possibly touch one of your sensitive spots. It is this, that newspaper commentators, who are not always the best-informed people on technical matters of theology, misinterpreted the statement of the Second Vatican Council on the Jews as equivalent to a forgiveness; that is to say, it was supposed that by it Catholics were now *forgiving* Jews for the portion of Jewish responsibility for the crucifixion (popularly called "deicide"). There were, of course, those of us who retorted to the newspaper reports of "forgiveness" that we Jews scarcely needed exculpation of what we have not been guilty of. The Vatican Declaration makes no mention of "forgiveness"; its intent, rather, is to provide a reliable guide for Catholics respecting Jews to replace what the Catholics have come to regard as wrong guides and wrong attitudes. The document does not suppose that the Catholic attitude has really *changed,* but only that the correct attitude has been *obscured* or *ignored* or *trespassed against.*

Respecting deicide, the premodern Christian view held that we Jews, all of us, were guilty of the death of Jesus; for that reason our Jewish scholars went to what I regard as an extreme in denying that any Jews *at all* had anything *at all* to do with it. To my mind, unclear as are the historical facts, it would have been quite natural for some individual Jews to have been involved; indeed, it would be understandably human if that were the case. It used to be the Christian tendency to hold the Romans completely innocent, and to allege that all of us Jews, of then, of now, and of the future, inherit guilt for the death of Jesus; this is an attitude which we Jews have naturally not taken to. It is scarcely to be believed that guilt can be bequeathed from one generation to another. Similarly, respecting your past persecutions of us, I cannot see how we Jews can attribute an inherited guilt for past Christian persecutions to you innocent Christians of today. If you, living today, have done nothing, then obviously there is nothing for which to forgive you.

Very recently a new book by Charles Y. Glock and Rodney Stark entitled *Christian Beliefs and Anti-Semitism,*[9] provided the results of the survey made by these two non-Jewish professors of the University of California at Berkeley. It is their conclusion that "at least one-fourth of America's anti-Semites have a Christian religious basis for their prejudice, while nearly another fifth have this religious basis in considerable part. Indeed, only 5 per cent of Americans with anti-Semitic views lack all rudiments of a religious basis for their prejudice." This passage, and some related and similar ones, stirred up a minor controversy about its accuracy, and about the reliability of the relationship between the data the authors assembled and the conclusions they drew. By and large the general opinion seems to be that the facts and the conclusions are tenable. To Jewish and Christian leaders alike, these results seem to have constituted both a bewilderment and a shock. I personally did not respond in this way,

[9] New York, 1966.

for I can say that I would have imagined the situation to be somewhat along the lines which the quoted passage depicts. The bewilderment and shock are to be explained by the circumstance that Christian leadership is significantly free of anti-Jewish hostility and has attributed this freedom from it to all Christians, while Jewish leaders with a close relationship to Christian leaders similarly extended the favorable attitudes they have experienced to all Christians. The continued existence of anti-Jewish attitudes in some portions of Christendom (and of an analagous Jewish hostility to all Christians) is simply a fact of life that we Jews have had to learn to live with. Its eradication, should that ever come about, is a Christian concern, not a Jewish concern.

It is essential that we Jews not attribute to all Christians the unfortunate attitudes of some, or blame all of them for the character blemishes of only a portion of them. Our Jewish attitude to Christians must rest on what Judaism has taught and teaches, and must not be a response in its substance to large or small manipulations of hostility to us by Christians. Since we are human, we will, of course, respond in a normal human way to things which sear us. But our Jewish imperative must rise above any tendency to return hostility with hostility.

The Futility of Grievance

I have heard that some German youths, born after Hitler, asked a German theologian whether or not they bore the guilt for what their parents had done. His reply was that they could not inherit guilt; what they might inherit is a sense of shame, which could well lead to the determination that such things should not recur. Though I personally never suffered from Hitler, and my military service was in the South Pacific area and not in Europe, I am of an age that Hitler and what he did remains a major trauma to me, one from which I will never recover. I admit to a confusion of emotions about Germany and Germans.

Twice in Scripture there appears a proverb which is cited there to deny its validity: "The fathers have eaten sour grapes, and the teeth of the children have been set on edge." It occurs in Jeremiah 31:29 and Ezekiel 18:2; the continuation in Ezekiel (18:3) is worth noting: "As I live, says the Lord God, you will have no occasion any more to use this proverb in Israel." How German youth responds to the memory and the shame of the events of Hitler's time is their concern; it is my concern that I shall not hold them responsible for what they did not do.

Indeed, as someone whose major pursuit has been the study of the past, especially as Judaism and Christianity have confronted each other within it, I have come to see that the major importance of such study (beyond study for its own sake) is the possible guidance that the past can have for the present and the future. I have no great interest in raking up past grievances and in perpetuating them, and I know only one outcome to vindictiveness and that is that it breeds countervindictiveness. In my own approach, I see nothing about guiltless Christians to occasion a meaningless "forgiveness." I see a residue of unclear matters about the present, and bases for honest people to differ in judgment as to what to do, but I remain hopeful that greater, even full clarity can emerge. My predominant concern is the future. We Jews and you Christians need to confront each other in the light of today, and not carry over the misfortunes of the past.

8

THE FUTURE: THE JEWISH CHOICE

We Jews have no intention of dissolving our Judaism. To the contrary, we are committed to perpetuating it and to deepening it. We consider it to have values not only for us, but through us for all mankind. Accordingly, we shall continue to maintain our congregations, and build our synagogues, and educate our children in Judaism.

When we Jews lived in periods of adversity, we ordinarily knew exactly what to do and how. We find ourselves, now that adversity has largely given way to a hospitable environment, in considerable perplexities, and often we face questions for which we find no ready answer. We want to live in open communities, and we insist in being part of Western culture; yet the open community creates erosions among us. Some of our people leave us, just as some of your people leave Christianity. Often those who leave us do not go to you, but go rather to the religious no-man's land which has grown so large in the Western world. Since we send our children to the same secular schools to which you send yours and they meet more freely in "after-hours" social activity than their parents do, it is inevitable that some of our children will want to marry each other. Both your tradition and ours have frowned on such marriages, and in some ages both traditions have prohibited them. Today they can no longer be prohibited; they can only be discouraged. If the clergy among you or among us abstain from presiding or officiating at the marriage ceremony (as happens), then the youngsters have recourse to a civil official, and they can ignore a view among some of you which supposes that such a marriage is less than valid, or among us that it is only reluctantly valid. You who are Catholics have set certain preconditions to the marriage of a Catholic to a Protestant, while you Protestants have usually abstained from such preconditions, but have resented the Catholic preconditions. Among us Jews there has existed, and still exists, a view which regards the marriage of a Jew to a Gentile, without regard to conditions or preconditions, as an act of apostasy, and such a Jew will mourn his intermarrying son or daughter as if dead. Others among us Jews have created sets of "preconditions" somewhat similar to the Catholic preconditions. Among still others of us, by far the minority, there exists no sense of objection to intermarriage. The majority among us, at least so I think, regard a marriage between a Jew and a convert to Judaism as a marriage between two Jews, and hence such conversion has come to attend a certain number of intermarriages. In some cities, since the number of such contemplated marriages has been growing, there are classes held to instruct Gentiles in Judaism as a prelude to conversion and to marriage.

While there have been situations in which we as Jews have objected to intermarriage with Christians, this has been an objection to intermarriage with Gentiles rather than with Christians as such. The objection has been to marriage "outside the fold" rather than to the religion of the person outside. Such objection has been a part of the Jewish religion, but it reflects inevitably the tendency of Jews to practicality, and therefore is concerned with the question: Will the marriage work? Will the person, on marrying a Jew, be prepared for the peculiarities of social exclusions, of separate social systems, and be prepared, God forbid, for those discriminations and persecutions which still exist? As far as my limited observation has gone, such questions have a greater priority among us than the questions of the other aspects of the personal character of the person outside the fold. It seems to me that neither I nor any other Jew has an answer to the perplexity of intermarriage. It is a fact that our pulpit has consistently advocated against it, often on purely social grounds rather than religious ones; our statisticians report, nevertheless, a constant rise in the frequency of it.

I mention intermarriage only as an example of some of our perplexities today, especially in our desire to perpetuate our Judaism. If we were prepared to dissolve Judaism, most of these problems would automatically disappear. The general tenor of our unsolved problems relates to our wish, on the one hand, to remain an entity, a corporate religious body, and, on the other hand, to participate as individuals in the open community of our time. But despite our desire not to be separated from the culture of the modern world, we have not solved the problem of the extent to which we want to retain aspects of our traditional separateness. We sometimes quarrel among us about the legitimacy of some of our separate institutions, such as a Jewish hospital, or a Yeshiva or Brandeis University, or a Jewish country club; and usually these quarrels exhibit preconceptions which stand in the way of minds confronting each other on the same level, and often theoretical positions are inconsistent with the realities. (I have heard Jews say: "On principle I am against a Jewish country club, but I belong for the simple reason that the *Goyim* ['Gentiles'] won't take me in.")

To what extent we Jews shall be able to steer through the confusions of the time in perpetuating our Judaism, and still participate in the flow of modern civilization, seems to me very much uncertain. There are moments in which I wonder whether or not Judaism will withstand the erosion which modern civilization offers, especially since I see Christianity equally in jeopardy. Indeed, its status as a majority may well predispose it, simply because it is the majority religion, to an even greater erosion than we may undergo.

How I wish it were possible that those of us who do not want to be Jews could find some way of leaving us! They would be happier, and so would we. For to us to whom Jewishness is a set of affirmative values, the gain of remaining Jewish is well worth the cost, and the debit in the form of discrimination well worth the credit, in the form of preserving something we cherish as precious to us and as advantageous to mankind.

Universal Religion

The Judaism which I personally wish to preserve appeals to me as a religion of universal relevance. I live in a particular state, Ohio, and vote in it; I express my American patriotism through the vehicle of my Ohio residency. Ohio is the particular, but the nation, indeed mankind, is the universal. Judaism is my particular, through which I express my universals.

I think I am aware of facets of our corporate Jewish existence that I would change if I could. Indeed, I love my tradition deeply enough to be critical of it at points. But I know also its great depth and its tremendous moments and achievements. It is from a Jewish source, the literature of the pre-exilic prophets, that there emerged the first visions of a united humanity living in a world of universal peace. I cannot turn my back on this. I am sure that other Jews feel the same commitment with equal earnestness.

We Jews intend to remain Jews. Your Jewish neighbor intends to remain a Jew. We Jews welcome converts who seek us out; we do not go out seeking for converts, though perhaps we should. Your Jewish neighbor will in all probability send his children to a Jewish religious school, whether an all-day parochial school (which most of us Jews seem opposed to), or an afterschool school (which most of our children find burdensome) or a Sunday school (which almost all of us consider insufficient as a vehicle).

What does your Jewish neighbor want of himself respecting you? What does he want of you? The answer to both questions is the same: a good neighbor.

Two hundred years ago he could not have been your neighbor, nor you his. Two hundred years ago he was inevitably regarded as your enemy, and you his.

All this is in the process of change, and the change is already far advanced. What was not possible then is possible now.

Possible, but less than certain. Possible, but fraught with misunderstandings aggravated by occasionally excessive sensitivities. Possible, but shadowed by the traumas of the past tragic decades and by unwholesome incidents.

Possible, already in our time. And who knows what even greater blessing the future might bring if each of us tries earnestly to learn and understand?

9

A PROPOSED DECLARATION: "THE SYNAGOGUE AND THE CHRISTIAN PEOPLE"

The Synagogue views the Christian people as among its offspring. It acknowledges that Christian people have laudably spread the message of the Synagogue among people and in areas of the world beyond where the Synagogue had penetrated. The Christian people have adapted that message to their own character and their own ways of thinking and speaking, and they have both preserved much which is familiar to the Synagogue and also created much which is not. Man, in his weakness, has been incapable of maintaining unbroken unity. Neither the Synagogue nor the church has been free from division, and a by-product of such division has been irreligious hatred, bitter recrimination, and persecution, both within and without. Since hatred, recrimination, and persecution are irreligious, the Synagogue laments all such manifestations within its past, and respecting the present and the future repudiates them as inauthentic manifestations of the spirit of Judaism. The Synagogue holds that its message must spread not by power or by might, but only by the Spirit of God and in the love of mankind.

The Synagogue is aware that Christian assemblies, lamenting and disavowing the Christian persecution of the Jews, have spoken in recent times in the same vein. The Synagogue welcomes these pioneer utterances.

All men are wont to remember grievances out of which attitudes of vindictiveness arise; therefore the Synagogue reminds its loyal sons of the biblical injunction (Leviticus 19:18): "Thou shalt not take vengeance nor bear any grudge against the children of thy people but thou shalt love thy neighbor as thyself." The Synagogue cannot, and does not, hold innocent Christians of our day responsible for the persecutions of the past, nor all Christians responsible, in the present or the future, for the misdeeds which may come from some.

The Synagogue continues to look forward to that day when all men, of all countries, colors, and beliefs, will become spiritually united. Since all universals are attained only through particulars, the Synagogue is committed to the perpetuation of itself against all forms of dissolution. It understands "the election of Israel" as imposing on it a heavier obligation to God, not as an unseemly preferment. It welcomes into its midst all those who voluntarily wish to enter. It does not seek to dissolve the institutions of its offspring, nor does it cherish, as a proximate or remote goal, the abandonment by Christians of their Christian loyalties. Rather, it desires that its offspring attain and maintain the spiritual heights which they often nobly expressed.

The Synagogue envisages the unity of mankind in a lofty spiritual bond, enabling men both to preserve the institutions which they hold sacred and to transcend them.

A frank, fair and [illegible]
revealing book. However, I
continue to be appalled at
his lack of knowledge of the
Evangelical community. Unaware
that...

1. Decade totally foreign to
evangelical thought
2. Vocation a Catholic Not
Protestant Concept.
3. Evangelicals have Jewish
tradition.

Tends to treat this area in
oversimplified terms.